THEIR GOD IS TOO SMALL

THEIR
GOD
IS TOO
SMALL

OPEN THEISM AND THE UNDERMINING OF CONFIDENCE IN GOD

Bruce A. Ware

CROSSWAY BOOKS

A DIVISION OF
GOOD NEWS PUBLISHERS
WHEATON, ILLINOIS

Their God Is Too Small: Open Theism and the Undermining of Confidence in God

Copyright © 2003 by Bruce A. Ware

Published by Crossway Books
        a division of Good News Publishers
        1300 Crescent Street
        Wheaton, Illinois 60187

Cover design: Josh Dennis

First printing 2003

Printed in the United States of America

Library of Congress Cataloging-in-Publication Data
Ware, Bruce A.
   Their God is too small : open theism and the undermining of
confidence in God / Bruce A. Ware.
     p. cm.
   Includes bibliographical references and indexes.
   ISBN 1-58134-481-3 (TPB : alk. paper)
   1. God—Omniscience. 2. Providence and government of God.
3. Free will and determinism—Religious aspects—Christianity.
I. Title.
BT131.W275   2003
231—dc21   2003007907

VP		13	12	11	10	09	08	07	06	05	04	03
15	14	13	12	11	10	9	8	7	6	5	4	3	2	1

CONTENTS

Introduction

FROM MY FIRST EXPOSURE to what is called the "open" view of God, I have wanted to help "set the record straight" concerning this new way of looking at God. I have wanted to do all I can to uphold the true character of our glorious God and the true faith we cherish as Christians in the face of this diminished view of both God and our faith. For the glory of God and for the good of Christian people, the open view needs to be seen for what it is and evaluated carefully by biblically-minded Christians. I am confident that when this evaluation has been done, followers of the true and living God will see the openness deity as an imposter and not the true God he is claimed to be.

The treatment of the open view in these pages is anything but exhaustive. Yet it provides a sufficient overview of and interaction with the position that readers will understand this movement's basic features along with some of its most serious problems. My longer and more sustained interaction with open theism is available in another Crossway publication, *God's Lesser Glory: The Diminished God of Open Theism*.

I write this book very much aware that significant portions of the evangelical movement are willing to validate the legitimacy of open theism. Major evangelical publishers and educational institutions have the view that open theism ought to be considered an "evangelical option" even if it is never widely accepted. I differ with this assessment. My own view is that open theism is both wrong and damaging to faith in ways that cannot rightly be tolerated in the evangelical church. Our day certainly is not known for its strong backbone or sharp boundary lines. To the contrary, we live in a era that likes to be defined more by what we hold in common in the center of our faith than by doctrines that distinguish us. On many issues where we differ, I also would strongly urge toleration and ongoing discussion. Open theism has deviated too far, however. This view of God is too small. The openness understanding of God belittles his glory and perfection, and its vision of faith leads to despair. We simply cannot stand by idly and allow the advocates of the openness view to influence the next generation of evangelicals unchallenged.

I wish to offer my thanks to the administration of The Southern Baptist Theological Seminary where I have the privilege to teach. Faculty writing projects are encouraged and supported, and I am grateful to serve in an institution where such work is valued. And I praise God for Crossway Books. In a day when some of our most respected Christian publishers are advancing various theological positions that represent distressing departures from our common faith, Crossway has shown a willingness and a desire to take a stand and support "the faith once for all given to the saints." My own family has, once again, prayed much for me throughout the writing process. Phone calls to my mom and dad, or to my sister, nearly always included their encouraging words and expressions of prayer for my writing. Only in heaven will we know just how much these words of encouragement and prayers effected. But I am grateful. And to my wife, Jodi, and to Bethany and Rachel, I wish to give my deepest thanks. Jodi has again borne with me under the pressures of long hours and late nights. Her support has never wavered. And my precious daughters' love for this dad means the world to me. I especially wish to thank Rachel for allowing me to tell some of her story in the pages of this book.

May God be pleased to advance the glory of his name and to buttress the faith and hope of his people. And to the extent that the critique offered here will assist in greater understanding of the true God and greater confidence in him, I will be the first to give God all the praise. For to him alone belongs all the glory, both now and forevermore. Amen.

1

OPEN THEISM AND THE CHRISTIAN FAITH

SETTING THE STAGE

Consider the following "Christianly" advice:

"God is a God of love, and as such, he respects you and your desires. He's not one to 'force' his way on another. So then, God isn't interested in planning out your future for you and giving you no say in what you do in your life! No, in fact, much of the future hasn't been planned yet, and God is waiting on you to make your decisions and choose your course of action so that he knows how best to make his own plans. Of course he wants you to consult him in the process, though what you decide will be your choice, not his. What God wants is for you and him to work together in charting out the course of your life. And you can be sure that he will do everything in his power to help you have the best life that you can."

Or consider this counsel:

"When tragedy intrudes into your life, please don't think that God had anything to do with it! God doesn't want pain and suffering to occur, and when it does, he feels as badly about it as those do who are suffering. And don't think that, somehow, this tragedy must fulfill some ultimately good purpose. It well may not! Evil happens all the time that God doesn't want, and often it serves no good purpose at all. But when tragedy does occur, we can trust God to be with us and help us rebuild what was lost. After all, one thing we know for sure, and that is that God is love. So, although he simply can't keep a whole lot of evil things from happening, he will be with us when they do happen."

Or again:

"God took a huge risk in creating a world with moral creatures who could use their freedom to go against what he desired and wanted to occur. All through history we see evidence of people (and fallen angels) using their God-given freedom to bring about horrific evil and causing untold pain and misery. Of course while God could not have known in advance what free creatures would do, surely he never has wanted *that* to happen! He is love, and he doesn't want his creatures to suffer. But one thing we can know for sure is that God will win in the end! So don't worry, because God will make sure that what he wants most badly to happen will be fulfilled. You can trust him with all your heart!"

These statements are all consistent with a relatively new movement within our evangelical churches called "open theism." This movement takes its name from the fact that its adherents view much of the future as "open" rather than closed, even to God. Much of the future, that is, is yet undecided, and hence it is unknown to God. God knows all that can be known, open theists assure us. But future free choices and actions, because they haven't happened yet, do not exist, and so God (even God) cannot know them. God cannot know what does not exist, they claim, and since the future does not now exist, God cannot now know it. More specifically, he cannot know, in advance, that large portion of the future which will come about as free creatures choose and do as they please. Accordingly, God learns moment-by-moment what we do, when we do it, and his plans must constantly be adjusted to what actually happens, insofar as this is different than what he anticipated.

WHY DO OPEN THEISTS BELIEVE WHAT THEY DO?

So, what can be said for the open view? That is, why would Christian people be attracted to this understanding of God? Let me suggest three main reasons that open theists would offer. First, those who hold an openness perspective believe that a relationship with God is much more vital and "real" when the God with whom we interact does not (and cannot) know in advance what we will do. After all, if God doesn't know what you're going to say or do or decide until you actually act, then he must wait and learn from you what you have chosen. Upon learning that, God can then interact with you on what you have decided, and your relationship can then resemble much more what we normally think of as a "real personal relationship." Granted, we all acknowledge that God knows much more than we do, says the open theist; after all, he knows the past and present perfectly. But if he knows the future perfectly also, then this turns our interaction with him into a sham. If God knows all of the future definitely and perfectly, then he knows (and always has known) every word that you will ever speak, every choice that you will ever make, and every action that you will ever perform. So what would God's response be to your choices and actions, if he knew them all in advance? God could never be truly surprised or delighted or grieved, or relate with you in "real ways," for he would always have to respond, "Yes, I knew you would say that," or, "Yes, I knew you would do that." No real relationship would be possible, open theists argue, if God knows all of our free choices and actions before we do them.

Second, when suffering and affliction come into our lives, open theists believe that their view of God is greatly comforting. Moreover, they think that their solution to the "problem of evil" is more satisfying than anything offered by a more traditional view of God. The open theist says you should always understand that God did not plan for suffering to come into your life. And he surely is not using it in your life to accomplish some hidden purpose. Rather, says the open theist, all evil comes about through the wrongful use of the free will that God has given his moral creatures. As Greg Boyd (a leading advocate of open theism) asserts, "The open view, I submit, allows us to say consistently in unequivocal terms that the ultimate source for all evil is found in the will of free agents rather than in God."[1] So there really is no "hidden agenda" behind suffering; God is not "secretly" bringing about your affliction. How do we know this? Because God is love and he simply wouldn't wish suffering on anyone. Often he doesn't even know just what affliction is coming or how severe it will be. And the fact remains, he doesn't want or will suffering to occur.

A natural question, then, is this: If God created the world, did he know that this unwanted suffering would be a part of the creation that he would make? And if so, what justifies God in creating a world containing the kinds of horrific suffering we experience? According to the open view, God did know that suffering would be a *possibility* in the world he created, but he did not know that it would *actually* occur. How is this? Well, simply, when God decided what kind of creation he would bring into existence, he chose for there to be "free" creatures. True freedom means, however, that while God wants people to use their freedom for good, he cannot give them the capacity for freedom and also control how they use it. This would be a contradiction, the openness proponent argues. So, in giving freedom, God accepts the possibility that people might use this good gift of freedom to bring about evil. Instead of using it to love, they might use it in hateful, hurtful, spiteful ways. God, then, knew unwanted evil was a possibility, but he just didn't know (until it happened) whether evil, in fact, would come about.

So how is God justified in creating a world he knew might contain evil? As long as he knew that the good that could come from freedom could have been accomplished only by giving the freedom itself with the possibility of it being used for evil, God is justified, say the open theists. In other words, the bare possibility of human freedom being used for good (which God expected would happen) provided justification for God to create a world in which he knew that evil *might* also come (as people used their freedom, wrongly, to do evil).

How is this a more satisfying answer to the "problem of evil" than the traditional answers of Christian theologians? Open theists argue that if (as traditionally believed) God knew the complete future of the world before he created it, that is, if he knew every atrocity, every rape, every brutal murder, every malicious insult, every genocide, then it is unimaginable that he would have created *this* world. Surely, the evil of this world is not what God wanted, and God bemoans all specific instances of evil that occur. But the bottom line is this (according to open theists): God simply could not have known in advance that evil would occur, and would occur to the extent that it has occurred, and he never wills such evil to happen. Therefore, they feel that God is vindicated from charges that he bears responsibility, as Creator, for the evil in the world.

Third and last, open theists claim that their view better accounts for Scripture's own teaching about God. That is, although the open view has not been advocated by any portion or branch of the Orthodox, Roman Catholic, or Protestant church throughout history, the bold claim of open theists is that their view is, in fact, more biblical. We will interact with some of these biblical claims as we move through this book, but it might help here to give you just a couple of examples[2] of where open theists base their claim.

Consider Jeremiah 19:5. In this verse God denounces Israel's evil and idolatry in performing such wickedness which, he says, "I did not command or decree, *nor did it come into my mind*" (emphasis added). It appears from this statement (see also, Jer. 7:31 and 32:35) that God is ignorant of the actions Israel will do, such that when they do it, *only then* does this knowledge of their activity "enter" God's mind. Surely this shows, says the open theist, that God has not known in advance just what actions Israel actually will do, even if he has always known what they possibly might do. As Greg Boyd comments, if God actually knew exactly what Israel would do, yet he tells us here that their very actions had not entered his mind, this amounts to a clear "contradiction"![3] Far better, he says, to take the meaning of the passage at face value and acknowledge that God learns what these free and sinful Israelites do only when they actually do it. Then, but not before, does this knowledge "enter" God's mind.

Or consider the account of Jonah being sent to Nineveh to proclaim its impending judgment. After the reluctant prophet finally goes to Nineveh and preaches God's message, the Ninevites repent and plead for mercy. And then we read, "When God saw what they did, how they turned from their evil way, God relented of the disaster that he had said he would do to them, and he did not do it" (Jonah 3:10). Surely this indicates, says the open theist, that God planned one thing (namely, judgment) based on the sin and wickedness of Nineveh, but then when he learned that they had repented, God himself "repented" and changed his mind about what he had planned to do. How could God thus change his mind, asks the open theist, if he had already known exactly what the Ninevites would do? Does this change of mind not indicate that God does not know the entire future?

Open theism proposes, then, that it presents the nature of our relationship with God in more realistic ways than does traditional theology, that it provides a better answer to the existence of evil in our world, and that it is being more faithful to what the Bible actually teaches. If this is the case, why should we be concerned? Isn't open theism at least a possible correct understanding of what Scripture teaches, and shouldn't we accept this as a legitimate view, even if we don't agree fully with it? Why be concerned with what open theists are advocating?

WHY SHOULD WE BE CONCERNED?

Throughout this book we will examine a number of issues that raise deep concerns. But allow me to suggest two overarching concerns about open theism that should raise significant questions in the minds of Christians. First, the very *greatness, goodness, and glory of God are undermined* by the open view of God. While the open view tries to understand God as more "relational" and "really involved" in human affairs, the way it does so is by portraying God as less than he truly is. Of the open view we cannot help but say, "Their God is too small!"

Think about it. Here we have a God who has to wait, in so many, many cases, to see what *we* will do before he can decide his own course of action. While this is a very natural way to think of *human* choice and action, does this rightly apply to the God of the Bible? The true and living God of the Bible proclaims, "I am God, and there is no other; I am God, and there is none like me, declaring the end from the beginning and from ancient times things not yet done, saying, 'My counsel shall stand, and I will accomplish all my purpose'" (Isa. 46:9b-10). Surely such a majestic God stands high and exalted and far above the proposed God of the open view. The Bible's abundant prophecies, most of which involve innumerable future free human choices and actions, should be enough by themselves to indicate that the true God does not have to wait to see what we do before he makes up his mind. If God doesn't know what we will do before we do it, how could Christ, for example, warn Peter that before the rooster crowed, Peter would deny him three times (John 13:38)? Was this a good guess on Jesus' part? Hardly! Recall that just a few verses earlier in John 13 Jesus had told the disciples that he would begin telling them things before they take place so that when they occur, "you may believe that I am he" (John 13:19). God knows in advance what we will do, and he can, when he wishes, declare it to us as evidence of his very deity. The open view brings God down, pure and simple. It tries to give more significance to human choice and action at the expense of the very greatness and glory of God. The God of open theism is too small, simply because he is less than the majestic, fully knowing, altogether wise God of the Bible.

One more example may help us see how the open view undermines the true portrayal of God in Scripture. In open theism, because God often makes his plans not knowing exactly how things will work out (after all, he can't predict exactly what his moral creatures will do in light of the actions he performs), it may be the case that God actually looks back on *his own past actions* and concludes that what *he did* was not best. A striking example of this is found in John Sanders's *The God Who Risks,* in which Sanders discusses the account of the flood (Genesis 6–8). Because of the rainbow and God's pledge never to flood the earth again, Sanders suggests that here God reconsiders whether he actually should have brought the flood, and its painful judgment, on the world in the first place. Sanders writes, "It may be the case that although human evil caused God great pain, the destruction of what he had made caused him even greater suffering. Although his judgment was righteous, God decides to try different courses of action in the future."[4] In other words, we are left with the very uneasy and deeply distressing notion that even God (as is often true for us humans) may look back on his own past actions and say, "While this was just, it may not have been best!" Such a view of God calls into question God's very wisdom and the flawless goodness of both his character and actions. Can we count on God to do, always and only, what is best? If the open view is true, the answer must be no. Again, it should be apparent to Bible-believing Christians that the open view of God diminishes God's full integrity, wisdom, greatness, goodness, and glory. Their God is just too small.

Second, *the strength, well-being, faith, hope, and confidence of Christian people in and through their God are undermined* by the open view. To see just how devastating to true Christian faith the open view is, consider for a moment one of the most cherished passages and promises in all the Bible: "Trust in the LORD with all your heart, and do not lean on your own understanding. In all your ways acknowledge him, and he will make straight your paths" (Prov. 3:5-6). What happens to these admonitions and assurances if the God of open theism is considered to be the true God? For one thing, the extent to which we can place our full trust in God, simply put, is demolished. Yes, the God of open theism will always *want* our best, but since he may not in fact *know* what is best, it becomes impossible to give him our unreserved and unquestioning trust. What if we trust him in his leading, for example, but begin experiencing hardships? What are we to conclude? Can we say with confidence, "These hardships are all part of the plan God has for me by which his good purposes will be accomplished"? If the God in whom we trust is the openness God, the answer must be a resounding no. Instead, when hardships come, the natural and unavoidable question of our anxious soul will be, "Did God anticipate these hardships when he gave me the direction that I have followed? Is it possible that the path I'm on is not really for my best, even though God might have thought it was earlier? And might it not be better to follow a different course than the one God directed me to take?" Just how are we to trust in the Lord with *all of our hearts* when we have doubts about God's ability to lead and direct in the best way?

Further, just how will we be inspired to acknowledge God and his wisdom and purposes in all of our ways, or have confidence that the paths he puts us on are "straight"? Whatever "straight paths" means in Proverbs 3:6, surely it indicates that the path you take will fulfill what God knows is best for your life. As we all know, the "straight" paths of God may have many twists and turns unanticipated by us. But from God's perspective, these paths are nonetheless "straight" because they actually fulfill exactly what God knows is best. Consider

Joseph, despised by his brothers, sold into Egypt, falsely accused by Potiphar's wife, thrown into prison—yet all that occurred, we are told, was part of God's plan (Gen. 50:20). Because Joseph is so sure of God's leading in all that happened in his life, he can say to his brothers, "It was not you who sent me here, but God"! (Gen. 45:8). But if, as open theism claims, God doesn't know what will happen in much of the future, and if God may find out that things have not gone as he intended, then it simply cannot be the case that God can rightly promise us that as we acknowledge him in all we do, he will ensure that our paths are "straight." But be clear on this: God—the true and living God of the Bible—*does* in fact make this astonishing, faith-inspiring, confidence-building, human-humbling promise! He *does* tell his children to trust him unreservedly, because he knows all that will occur and he promises to oversee everything in our lives as we keep our hope fixed exclusively on him! Our paths, as God's children, will be "straight," according to God's perfect and unassailable plan, as we place our faith and hope in him. But, sadly, nothing of the sort can be true with respect to the God of open theism. Again the assessment must be: their God is too small.

WHERE TO GO FROM HERE

The purpose of this book is to help thoughtful Christian people comprehend more clearly what happens to our understandings of God and of the Christian life if we accept the open view of God. Clearly, the proponents of open theism are commending their view as both biblical and enhancing of our understanding of how we should live as Christians. But it is my deep conviction, and the conviction of many other evangelicals, that the open view distorts the Christian portrayal of God and his relations with his people so much

21

that open theism must not be viewed as "just another" legitimate Christian understanding. In other words, this issue is not like our differences over questions of the nature of the millennium and the timing of the return of Christ, or of whether all of the charismatic gifts have continued to this day or not, or of whether we should advocate believer's baptism or bring the infant children of believers to the baptismal font. No, the open view of God represents a departure from the church's uniform understanding of Scripture and a distortion of the biblical portrayal of God. To allow this as a legitimate view is essentially to allow the worship of a different God than the God of the Bible.

For some readers, this may sound like an overstatement, but I am convinced it is not. Recall that the true God challenged the false gods of the pagan nations surrounding Israel to "prove" their supposed deity, and the test he gave them was this: "Tell us what is to come hereafter, that we may know that you are gods" (Isa. 41:23a). Because these pagan gods had not predicted what was taking place, and because they were unable to tell what was coming afterwards, God's own judgment of them is telling: "Behold, they are all a delusion; their works are nothing; their metal images are empty wind" (Isa. 41:29). Furthermore, God's indictment of those false gods and those who worship them is striking: "Behold, you [gods] are nothing, and your work is less than nothing; an abomination is he who chooses you" (Isa. 41:24).

Is it too harsh, then, to say that the open view of God is unacceptable as a legitimate evangelical option? I do not think so, when it is clear that the one criterion by which God rejected the pretender deities of Isaiah's day is the same criterion by which the "God" of open theism may be tested and found wanting. The true God knows the future, can predict it accurately, and can state exactly what will take place, including innumerable future free human actions and events. And when things happen just as God said, we know that he is God. Because the "God" of open theism does not know most of the future of humankind, because he cannot declare what his creatures will or will not do, and because Scripture places this as a test for true deity, it is clear that the God of open theism is not the God of the Bible. Both the belittling of God and the harm done to Christian people through this view of God demand that we understand better just why we must say no to the openness proposal. As is evident in so many ways, affecting so many areas of life and theology, their God is just too small!

The chapters that follow will try to show more clearly in certain areas of our common faith and the Christian life just where the open view of God falters. Along the way, we will surely notice legitimate concerns that openness proponents raise that must be addressed. But the pattern that will clearly emerge is this: if Christians work from the understanding and theology that the open view of God proposes, we end up with biblical, theological, and practical problems of such a magnitude that the view itself must be called into question in its entirety. Here, then, is a brief overview of the areas we will cover and what we hope to see in these chapters.

Chapter 2 begins where we should begin, with a consideration of what Scripture teaches about God and his knowledge of the future. I will attempt to show that the open view is deeply flawed in its attempts to account for Scripture's own teaching about both God and his foreknowledge. Because this is a large topic, and because I have written at length on it elsewhere,[5] I propose here to offer some responses to key openness arguments, followed by selective meditations on other biblical passages and teachings, all with the goal of establishing the clarity and forcefulness with which Scripture teaches God's exhaustive and definite knowledge of the future.

Chapter 3 will dive right into one of the areas that open theists argue commends their view to the Christian community, namely, the problem of suffering and evil. Even though openness advocates claim that the open view deals much better with problems of suffering and affliction than does any traditional understanding, we will see that this simply is not the case.

Chapter 4 takes up the practice of prayer in the Christian life. Here, too, openness proponents claim that praying to a God who faces an open future makes prayer real and vital. We will examine this claim and notice some of the problems the Christian is left with if he moves in an openness direction.

Chapter 5 will ask what sort of hope we can rightly have in the God of open theism. While the true God wants his people to hope in him alone, both for life now and for eternity, the God of open theism undermines such hope and robs Christian people of the confidence to know that God's purposes will not fail and his plans will not falter.

Having read this digest of the problems attendant on the open view, the reader will, I hope, be in a better position to behold the greater glory and majesty of the true and living God. I hope the reader will also see, quite clearly, that the God of open theism is just too small to be the God of the Bible.

2

OPEN THEISM AND
GOD'S FOREKNOWLEDGE

BIBLICAL SUPPORT OFFERED FOR THE
OPEN VIEW OF GOD'S FOREKNOWLEDGE

Does Scripture teach that God does not know the future exhaustively? In particular, what about the future decisions and actions that we human beings make all the time—such as what I might choose to say next or what you might choose to do with another person tomorrow or where someone else might choose to travel next summer? Is it true that God cannot know what these will be until we do them? Open theists not only believe that this must be the case in order for our human decisions and actions to be truly free, they also claim that this is just what the Bible leads us to conclude.

For proponents of the open view, there are a number of indications in the Bible that God learns from what happens. Some passages, they say, indicate that God grows in knowledge as he observes *what* people do, *when* they do it. For example, there is the incident when God tested Abraham, asking him to offer up his only son, Isaac. When Isaac was bound and Abraham was about to plunge the knife into him, the angel of the Lord stopped Abraham and said, "Do not lay your hand on the boy or do anything to him, for now I know that you fear God, seeing you have not withheld your son, your only son, from me" (Gen. 22:12). Clearly, says the open theist, this shows that God learned something about Abraham from this very test. As John Sanders's observes, "God needs to know if Abraham is the sort of person on whom God can count for collaboration toward the fulfillment of the divine project. Will he be faithful? Or must God find someone else through whom to achieve his purpose?"[1]

Other passages, say the open theists, indicate that God sometimes realizes that events have unfolded differently than he expected they would. For example, in 1 Samuel 15 we hear God twice say that he "regretted" making Saul king (1 Sam. 15:11, 35). What possible sense does it make, ask the open theists, to say that God regrets how Saul acted as king if, as the traditional view holds, he knew all along exactly what Saul would do as king? In other words, can God really regret some action of his that he has known for all eternity would work out exactly as it did? Commenting on this passage, Greg Boyd says:

> We must wonder how the Lord could truly experience regret for making Saul king if he was absolutely certain that Saul would act the way he did. Could God genuinely confess, "I regret that I made Saul king" if he could in the same breath also proclaim, "I was certain of what Saul would do when I made him king"? I do not see how. . . . Common sense tells us that we can only regret a decision we made if the decision resulted in an outcome other than what we expected or hoped for when the decision was made.[2]

It seems clear, therefore, to advocates of the open view that God had certain hopes and expectations about Saul that didn't turn out as God had planned and thought they would. When Saul proved to be a dis-obedient king, God realized that his hopes for Saul simply were not true. And having learned this about Saul, God then regretted mak-ing Saul king. God learned something he had not known previously: just what sort of king Saul *really* turned out to be.

A second example comes from the account of the flood. You'll recall that after the water subsided and God called Noah, his family, and the animals to come out of the ark, God put a rainbow in the sky as a sign of his promise that "the waters shall never again become a flood to destroy all flesh" (Gen. 9:15). As we have seen, although he is not certain of this, John Sanders wonders whether this promise might not indicate that God had reassessed his previous decision to kill all living things on the earth. God may have looked back on his own past actions and concluded that while what he did was just, per-haps this simply was not the best thing to do. Sanders comments:

> God makes a covenant with his creation that never again will vir-tually everything be annihilated. The sign of the rainbow that God gives is a reminder to himself that he will never again tread this path ([Gen] 9:14-16). It may be the case that although human evil caused God great pain, the destruction of what he had made caused him even greater suffering. Although his judgment was righteous, God decides to try different courses of action in the future.[3]

So, whether God looks back at the things humans do that turn out differently than he expected (e.g., the unexpected disobedient actions of Saul), or whether he looks back at his own actions and reassesses whether what he did was best (e.g., both making Saul king and flood-ing the entire earth), it seems clear to advocates of open theism that God learns from what happens. Part of what indicates this in

Scripture are times when God regrets what he has done and reassesses or changes his mind.

EVALUATING THE BIBLICAL CASE FOR THE
OPEN VIEW OF GOD'S FOREKNOWLEDGE

Should these and other such passages be interpreted as open theists interpret them? Should we rightly conclude that the Bible indicates that God's knowledge of the future is limited, and that he actually learns some of what happens only when free persons make their choices and carry out what they have freely chosen? Evaluation of this way of understanding the Bible involves two lines of response. First, we should look carefully at the passages used in support of the open view and see if they really indicate that, as history unfolds and people make their free choices, God truly learns what he did not know before. Second, we should ask whether the Bible in fact teaches that God knows what open theists say he cannot know, namely, future free human actions and choices. That is, does Scripture any-where teach that God knows (in advance) what free persons will choose to do?

Both of these lines of response are quite involved, and here we can look at only a small portion of the Bible's teaching.[4] Perhaps the clearest way to proceed would be, first, to respond at least to the three passages cited above that are used to support the open view. In the process, I will cite other passages used by openness advocates and give a brief response. Second, I will offer some brief meditations on some other passages that both teach and illustrate God's knowledge of future free decisions and actions of people. I hope the reader will see from this study that the openness insistence that Scripture teaches that God learns as people freely do what they choose is not at all clear from Scripture itself, and that, furthermore, other passages clearly indicate that God in fact does know amazing detail about the future, including what free persons will choose and do in both the near and distant future. In the end, Scripture does not teach what open theists claim, and the church should not be led to think that it does. Well, now to our brief review: first, looking at passages used to support the open view; and then, a selective look at some other passages indicating that God in fact knows what open theists deny of him.

Evaluating Passages Used to Support the Open View

First, let's consider again the Abraham story, with its statement, "for now I know that you fear God" (Gen. 22:12). Since the open theist wants us to take the passage at face value, I suggest we do that and notice what it says God supposedly learned at this moment. The angel doesn't say that God now knows that Abraham would be obedient to God's command, or that Abraham would actually raise his knife with the intent of killing his son. No, he says, "for now I know that you *fear God.*" I cannot help but ask, Doesn't God have good reason to know already that Abraham feared him?

Surely God knows the heart of every person (1 Chron. 28:9 and 1 Sam. 16:7), and God also knows all of Abraham's track-record of obedience. This point is especially significant when we notice in the New Testament how often Abraham is cited as such a strong man of faith. In Romans 4 Paul extols Abraham's faith in God concerning the promised son, even after it became physically impossible for either Sarah or Abraham to become a parent (see especially Rom. 4:18-22). And Hebrews 11 honors Abraham both for leaving his country to follow God (Heb. 11:8-10) and for offering up Isaac

(Heb. 11:17-19; cf. James 2:21-23). This last point is interesting, because Hebrews 11:19 specifically upholds Abraham's faith that God would bring Isaac back from the dead. Now, isn't it clear that *God knew* of Abraham's life of faith, and that even as Abraham ascended Mt. Moriah to offer Isaac, *God knew* Abraham's heart of trust in God, believing even that God would raise Isaac after he had killed him? So can it be that at the moment that the angel stops Abraham, God *really learns only now* that Abraham fears him? Much more likely is the notion that when we read "for now I know that you fear God," it means that God, at this very moment, *sees afresh and witnesses* the extraordinary act of faith Abraham expresses, and in this sense, God knows (again, and forcefully) what he has known long before, namely, that Abraham fears God.

Perhaps it is something like an occasion when a very caring and loving husband expresses again to his wife his deep love for her. Suppose he comes home from work and surprises her with plans for a get-away weekend. In this moment of excitement and closeness, he might tenderly ask her, "Honey, do you know, deep in your heart, right now, that I love you?" And she might say, "After what you've just done, I really know, right now, how much you love me." Would it be right to conclude from this brief exchange that only now, at this moment but not before, she learned what she did not know before about her husband's love for her? Clearly, no. Rather, the present experience brought a fresh witnessing and reaffirmation of her husband's love, so that *now she knows* afresh his love. At least this much should be clear: in light of the whole of the Bible's teaching, we should not accept the open theist interpretation of Genesis 22:12 that insists on affirming that God learned at this moment what he did not know previously, namely, that Abraham feared him.

Consider also how similar the statement of Genesis 22:12 is to another passage just a few chapters earlier. In Genesis 18, the Lord appears to Abraham as three men come to visit him (see Gen. 18:1-2). After a while, God decides to tell Abraham about the destruction he plans to bring upon Sodom and Gomorrah. Notice carefully the language used in this account, and how relevant it is to this debate with open theism. We read, "Then the LORD said, 'Because the outcry against Sodom and Gomorrah is great and their sin is very grave, *I will go down to see* whether they *have done* altogether according to the outcry that has come to me. And *if not, I will know*" (vv. 20-21, emphasis added). Open theists insist that language about God learning from what happens ought to be taken "literally" or in a "straightforward" manner.[5] Well, consider what we would end up with from this passage if we follow this openness approach. First, we would have to *deny that God is omnipresent* (i.e., everywhere present), because God says that he has to "go down to see" if what he has heard is true. This indicates, on a "straightforward" reading, that until God gets to Sodom, he cannot know whether the reports he has heard are correct. Second, we would have to *deny that God knows everything about the past,* for he has to confirm whether the Sodomites *have done* these horrible things. Evidently, then, God does not know whether what he has heard about their past actions is true, so he doesn't know the past perfectly. Third, we would have to *deny that God knows everything about the present.* Because he has to go down to see, God doesn't know right now whether the reports are true.

But here is the problem: all evangelical and orthodox Christians, even open theists, affirm that the God of the Bible 1) is omnipresent, 2) possesses perfect and exhaustive knowledge of the past, and 3) possesses perfect and exhaustive knowledge of the present. We all believe this because of the abundance of biblical teaching on all three of these points. So, is it not clear that we should interpret Genesis 18:20-21 as indicating something other than, *literally*, that God has to go to Sodom to know if what he has heard is true? Perhaps we should interpret this passage in a way similar to how we would interpret a father's statement to his little boy while playing hide-and-seek: "Well, let's look around the corner and see if your sister might be hiding there, and then we'll know." The father says this knowing all the while that she in fact is there. And if it is clear that we should not take Genesis 18:20-21 at face value, should we not consider also that the same kind of language is being employed four chapters later in Genesis 22:12? Clearly the case for the openness interpretation simply cannot be made from a text like this.

Second, what about God regretting that he had made Saul king (1 Sam. 15:11, 35)? Does this regret indicate that God thought one thing would happen (that Saul would be a good king), but now learns what he didn't know before, that something else has happened (that Saul turned out to be disobedient)? To answer this, consider how amazing it is that sandwiched between the two statements of God's regret over Saul is one of the strongest and clearest biblical affirmations that God *does not* regret things that happen (even using the *same word* in Hebrew for "regret" that is used in verses 11 and 35!): "And also the Glory of Israel will not lie or have regret, for he is not a man, that he should have regret" (1 Sam. 15:29). Do verses 11 and 35 contradict verse 29? How can God "regret" that he "made Saul king" (vv. 11, 35) and yet be a God who "will not lie or have regret" (v. 29)?

Two features of 1 Samuel 15:29 deserve brief mention. First, notice how the author links together the ideas of "will not lie" and "[will not] have regret." Since it is true that God *never* lies (2 Tim.

2:13; Titus 1:2; Heb. 6:18), and since these ideas are connected in 1 Samuel 15:29, is not "God *never* lies and *never* regrets" the most natural way to understand this passage? Second, notice that God is said to be *unlike* mere humans, who do regret. Clearly, sometimes we humans do things that we regret, but other times we don't. But isn't this exactly what open theists say God is like—God sometimes regrets what he has done (e.g., making Saul king, or flooding the world), but other times he doesn't regret what he has done (e.g., giving his Son to die for sin)? But if both humans and God act in this way, then how can this passage say that "[God] is not a man, that he should have regret"? Surely, the answer is that this cannot be the correct understanding of God, or of this passage. This passage teaches that, unlike humans who sometimes regret and sometimes don't regret, God *never* regrets.

So how does verse 29 fit with verses 11 and 35? Here's my suggestion: On the one hand, God never learns new information and is never surprised by things that happen, and so he can never (v. 29) regret (in a strong sense) things that happen due to (supposedly) learning that what he anticipated did not happen. On the other hand, as things unfold that he previously knew would come to pass, he can still be deeply dismayed and grieved over the sin that he now witnesses, and in this way he can "regret" (vv. 11 and 35, in a weak sense) that these things are happening. Amazingly, in the very same passage the author wants us to know two things about God. First, we are to know that in fact, just as God cannot ever lie, so God's knowledge is fixed and he cannot ever find out something that will cause him to second-guess, to question, or to regret what he has done. He is God, not man, and as God, he is above any "regret" in this strong sense (v. 29). But second, just because God does not ever question what is happening (since he knew it all previously), we should not conclude that he doesn't care about the sin that unfolds. He does! He is deeply dismayed at what Saul does as he witnesses the unfolding of what he previously knew would occur. And as God observes Saul's sin, he bemoans the disobedience and harm that Saul's actions reflect. So, he "regrets" (in a weak sense) Saul's kingship, even though he knew and planned all along what is actually transpiring.

It seems clear, then, that the author of this chapter of Scripture intends for us to see both of these truths about God. How wrong we would be if we took only one of them and denied the other, but how glorious is our understanding of God when we see the balance intended. Openness interpreters miss this balance, and in so doing, they diminish the greatness of this "Glory of Israel." The true God is not surprised by what occurs, but he cares deeply about the sin that unfolds. His ways are stable and his knowledge is perfect, but his concern for human actions is deeply genuine as well. What a glorious God, seen aright.

Third, how shall we understand the suggestion that God may have reconsidered his decision to bring a flood upon the whole world, concluding that this may not have been the best route to take (i.e., Sanders's interpretation of Gen. 9:12-16[6])? I see no other way to take this than as a suggestion that God in hindsight judged that he had made an enormous mistake. Granted, Sanders makes clear he believes that God was righteous in this judgment. Fine, but was he wise? Consider the magnitude of this mistake, if in fact God thought it so to be. The *whole world,* save a few people and animals, was deliberately killed by God in this action. Issues in human affairs could hardly get weightier than this. To think that God looked back and thought to himself, "This was too severe and I am not entirely sure that I should have done it," is nothing short of staggering! What confidence can we have in a God who must second-guess his own actions? What does this tell us about the wisdom of God's own plans? If God is not sure that what he does is best, can we be sure that he really knows what he is doing?

The simple fact is that a God who can only speculate regarding what much of the future holds, at times second-guesses his own plans, can get things wrong, and may even repent of his own past conduct is a God unworthy of devotion, trust, adoration, and praise. The openness interpretations of the passages they claim support their own view propose a God that just is too small to be the true and living God of the Bible. And besides, Scripture's abundant and clear teachings uphold an exalted view of the God who knows and declares "the end from the beginning" (Isa. 46:10), and to this biblical support we now give brief attention.

Biblical Support for God's Comprehensive and Definite Foreknowledge

Does Scripture teach that God knows the future completely as it will be, and that this includes his advance knowledge of what free persons will choose and do? The answer is yes! To see this, I will first present a sketch of the "big picture" about God, portrayed by Isaiah the prophet, especially in Isaiah 40–48. Here, we see the God who makes his own claim to deity on the basis that he knows, and tells, exactly what the future will be. Second, I will offer a short series of "meditations" on selected passages that show, clearly, that God knows exactly what open theists deny of him—that is, he knows in very specific instances and specific detail just what free persons will choose to do and carry out. Both the "big picture" and these individual meditations will demonstrate that God—the true and living God of the Bible—knows the future comprehensively and perfectly. We have good reason to put our hope and trust in this God, for nothing takes him by surprise. Behold, then, the greatness of our God!

ISAIAH'S "BIG PICTURE" OF GOD

We begin with Isaiah's vision of God's exhaustive foreknowledge. Have you heard of the old television show, "To Tell the Truth"? By asking questions of three different people, all portraying themselves as "Mr. Smith," the panelists would try to determine who was the real "Mr. Smith." Well, a similar question was faced in Isaiah's day: Who is the real God? And how shall we know that he is in fact God? In Isaiah 40–48, no fewer than nine separate sections[7] offer essentially the same argument, repeated in different ways but clearly for the same overall purpose: the true and living God, unlike imposter gods, can be known to be the true God because he alone can foretell exactly what the future will be. Someone might ask, How do you know God is God? Answer: The true God knows and declares the future.

Consider only two of these nine sections. In Isaiah 41:21-29, God challenges the false gods, the idols of the nations surrounding Israel, to prove that they are gods. And what is the test he puts forth? God declares, "Let them bring them [these imposter gods], and *tell us what is to happen. Tell us the former things,* what they are, that we may consider their outcome; or *declare to us the things to come. Tell us what is to come hereafter,* that we may *know that you are gods*" (Isa. 41:22-23a, emphasis added). Here we have the test, designed by God himself, for knowing whether or not you've got the true God. The true God has told things in the past that have come true so that we can "consider their outcome" and realize his deity. And the true God tells things now that will happen in the future, so that when they come about, "we may know" that he is God. Here, and in eight other sections in these chapters, God puts his own deity on the line and to the test. He says over and again, "You know that I am God because I, unlike the false gods, know and declare the future." How presumptuous and wrong, then, for some system of theology to come along and deny of God the very basis by which he asserts his own deity! Open theists run the risk of being charged, along with these false worshipers in Isaiah's day, of choosing a view of "god" that is an abomination in God's sight. Hear the sobering words of Isaiah 41:24 regarding the false gods who cannot declare the future, and those who worship them: "Behold, you [the false gods] are nothing, and your work is less than nothing; an abomination is he who chooses you."

A second passage from these chapters in Isaiah comes at Isaiah 46:8-11. Here, God says:

> Remember this and stand firm,
>   recall it to mind, you transgressors,
>   remember the former things of old;
> for I am God, and there is no other;
>   I am God, and there is none like me,
> declaring the end from the beginning
>   and from ancient times things not yet done,
> saying, "My counsel shall stand,
>   and I will accomplish all my purpose,"
> calling a bird of prey from the east,
>   the man of my counsel from a far country.
> I have spoken, and I will bring it to pass;
>   I have purposed, and I will do it.

Notice just two things. First, God connects his own deity with his claim to declare "the end from the beginning." The lead-up to this claim is remarkable: "I am God, and there is no other; I am God, and there is none like me." And who, pray tell, is this one-and-only God? None other than the One who declares all things that will be (i.e., the end from the beginning). So does it matter to God whether we think of him as the One who knows all the past, present, and future? Surely his claim to exclusive deity attached to his knowledge of all things from one end of history to the other shows just how much, in fact, it matters to him. He alone is God. He wants us to know this. And how we know it is by his demonstration of his knowledge of what will come to pass. We dare not deny of God what he offers as the basis for his claim (here again!) to exclusive deity.

Second, this passage indicates one future reality that clearly, indisputably, involves a host of future free choices and actions. For God says, "calling a bird of prey from the east, the man of my counsel from a far country" (46:11), speaking no doubt of the future kingly reign of Cyrus, named and foretold at the end of chapter 44 and beginning of chapter 45, who would be born and named nearly two hundred years after this prediction was made! And don't minimize just how much knowledge of the future this indicates. For God to know that Cyrus would be born, would be given this name, would be raised to be king, reign as a great king, conquer as king, and accomplish the specific things God says that he "anointed" (45:1) Cyrus to do, would require of God unimaginable foreknowledge of the host of free human actions associated with the successful rise and exploits of this specific person. The general claim of deity, that the true God knows "the end from the beginning" (Isa. 46:10), is here illustrated in one utterly remarkable prediction of the coming of "the man of my counsel." This is a man whose future God knows and who will accomplish God's will perfectly (Isa. 46:11). God is God; there is no other. And the true God knows the future exhaustively, and he predicts what he wishes in order to demonstrate and prove that his claim to exclusive deity is true.

Having seen this sketch from Isaiah of the "big picture" of God, let us now consider a selection of passages that offer specific teaching and illustration of God's knowledge of the future.

MEDITATION ON EXODUS 3:19-20

After appearing to Moses in the burning bush, but prior to the ten plagues and his delivering Israel through the Red Sea, the Lord speaks to Moses and says, "But I know that the king of Egypt will not let you go unless compelled by a mighty hand. So I will stretch out my hand and strike Egypt with all the wonders that I will do in it; after that he will let you go" (Ex. 3:19-20). This passage, interpreted most naturally and clearly, indicates that God certainly *knows* that the king of Egypt *will not* permit the children of Israel to go except under compulsion, and that God also *knows* that after he brings the plagues upon Egypt, the king *will* then let them go. That is, this is a declaration of God's knowledge of Pharaoh's future decisions, first to resist letting them go, then later, under compulsion, to let them go.

How do open theists, denying God's foreknowledge, attempt to account for such a passage? Essentially, they argue that predictions like this are probably "conditional."[8] That is, while these predictions look as though they state what God *will* do or what *will* happen, in actuality, whether the predictions are fulfilled (as stated) or not depends on certain unstated conditions. So, in this case, if Pharaoh remains stubborn and *never* lets the people go, or if he gives in *right away*—if one of these conditions were to arise—then God's stated predictions would not be fulfilled (for God had said that Pharaoh would at first resist but would then let the people go). But this is not a problem (say the open theists), because we are to understand that these predictions were made with these unstated conditions attached to them.

As a matter of principle, open theists are not wrong to appeal to such "conditional" predictions. Nearly all interpreters of Jonah, for example, agree that when Jonah predicted "Yet forty days, and Nineveh shall be overthrown!" (Jonah 3:4), we understand that an implied but unstated condition attached to this prediction: "unless you repent," this will happen. The people did repent, and God did not bring the predicted judgment. And nearly all agree that, even as Jonah knew, it was God's intent all along to show mercy to the Ninevites, knowing that the *stated prediction* of judgment would elicit their repentance so that God could then display his *originally intended mercy*.

But the question here in Exodus 3 is whether God's prediction to Moses should rightly be understood as a conditional prediction. I do not believe this text can be accounted for by appeal to "conditional prophecy" (for reasons I will give below). I believe, rather, that this text shows that God can know and can announce in advance just exactly what one of his free creatures will do in the future. If so, there are two options in regard to the openness proposal: 1) admit that the Bible teaches truth that conflicts fundamentally with open theism, or 2) continue to hold the openness model but say that in this case God worked in Pharaoh to override his freedom, so that Pharaoh did what God caused him (apart from his free will) to do. Neither option is desirable for open theists, so this leads us to consider the proposed solution that some open theists have offered to account for this text, namely that it is a conditional prophecy. What of this?

In a recent public e-mail, open theist Chelsea DeArmond offers this possible explanation of Exodus 3:19-20:

> Why not interpret this prophecy just like classical theists interpret God's prophesied destruction of the Ninevites due to their great wickedness against Israel—in other words, as a conditional prophecy? Like the Ninevites, Pharaoh could have responded to the first plague with prayer, fasting, and repentance, rather than hardening his heart. We would not therefore conclude that God was "wrong" about Pharaoh, just as we do not therefore conclude that God was "wrong" about the Ninevites when he did not destroy them as he prophesied he would.[9]

Consider, however, these reasons for thinking that Exodus 3:19-20 is a clear and unambiguous prediction of what God *knows* Pharaoh will do, both before and after God brings the plagues upon Egypt, and not a conditional prophecy which may or may not have been fulfilled as God had said.

1. *Argument from God's hardening of Pharaoh's heart to prevent him from letting Israel go.* In Exodus 4:21 God says that he will *harden Pharaoh's heart so that he will not let the people go.* If, however, Pharaoh had decided to let them go, then it would show that God had failed to accomplish what he said he would do (i.e., God would not have succeeded in hardening Pharaoh's heart). The stakes for God are raised, in other words, when he says not only that Pharaoh will not let the people go (3:19), but also that he will *harden Pharaoh's heart* so that he will not let them go (4:21). Add to this (as the narrative unfolds) that after Pharaoh hardens his own heart several times, God

then hardens Pharaoh's heart (cf. 9:12; 10:1, 20; 11:10) precisely so that he would not, as of yet, let the people go. This makes the earlier prediction of 3:19 sound less like a conditional prophecy, in which case Pharaoh could have actually decided to let them go (contrary to the stated words of both 3:19 and 4:21), and more like a certain prediction (3:19) that God ensures will be carried out (4:21). Granted, in itself, this argument will not carry the day, but it does raise a clear red flag of sorts, that the "conditional prophecy" proposal is at least very strained.

2. *Argument from the centrality of the Passover, occurring as a part of the tenth (last) plague.* Exodus 4:23 records God's continued words to Moses that he should tell Pharaoh, "Behold, I will kill your son, your firstborn." This adds a more specific prediction of what God says he will do, which makes a conditional-prophecy interpretation even less likely. After all, consider this. Just what is God predicting in 4:23? Isn't this a prediction about the last plague, when the Lord passes over the houses of the obedient Israelites who have sprinkled blood on their door posts but brings death to all the houses of the land of Egypt? Now consider just how important this "Passover" is in biblical theology. Consider how much it matters to God that he be shown as the One who "passed over" the houses with the blood but brought death to all those not covered by the blood. Do you think God cares whether or not he is able to demonstrate this saving act by passing over the Israelite homes? Is it possible that, following DeArmond's logic, "Pharaoh could have [again] responded . . . with prayer, fasting, and repentance, rather than hardening his heart," so that the last plague (instituting the Passover) would not have occurred? How likely is it that this prediction in 4:23 is merely conditional, in light of how much rests on God completing *all* the plagues, particularly the

tenth and last plague? Therefore, when God says in Exodus 3:19-20 that the king will let Israel go only after he stretches out his hand, does not God have in mind the Passover, and does this not preclude the possibility that Pharaoh would repent after the first (or even the ninth!) plague? Surely, the best and only contextually satisfying interpretation of 3:19-20 is that God predicted what he certainly *knew* Pharaoh would do, planning to deliver Israel only at the end of the full ten plagues.

3. *Argument from the plagues as the means by which God declares that he alone is Lord.* Consider again the prediction of Exodus 3:20, that God will stretch out his hand, and only after that will Pharaoh let Israel go. Now read Exodus 7:3-5, where God repeats (as he does several times) that he will harden Pharaoh's heart, multiply his signs, and *only then* will Israel be delivered. Now, of course, if Pharaoh had repented after the first sign (a possibility if this were a conditional prophecy), God would not have done what he said he would do, namely, he would not have multiplied his signs to compel Pharaoh to let the people go. Does it matter whether 3:19-20; 7:3-5; and the other predictive passages state what God *knows* will occur, or whether they are conditional prophecies that might not occur? In light of 7:5, the answer is, "Yes, it matters!" Here, God says, "The Egyptians shall know that I am the LORD, when I stretch out my hand against Egypt and bring out the people of Israel from among them." This is the immediate prelude to the beginning of the ten signs (plagues) that start in 7:14. The point is clear: God manifests his rightful deity ("I am the LORD") on the basis of his multiplying these signs, only after which Israel is delivered. Now, given that this great purpose (demonstrating that "I am the LORD") is accomplished through (and only through) these plagues, how likely

is it that God's prediction back in 3:20 is conditional (i.e., that Pharaoh might repent and let the Israelites go without God's "miracles" being manifested)? Again, the only contextually satisfying interpretation is that the prediction of 3:19-20 relates to things that God *will* do to manifest that he alone is God.

4. *Argument from the fulfillment of these predictions, "as the LORD had said."* Notice the use of the crucial phrases, "as the LORD had said," and, "just as the LORD had spoken through Moses" (7:13; 8:15, 19; 9:12, 35) throughout the plague narrative. Exodus 7:13 (after the first sign) says, "Still Pharaoh's heart was hardened, and he would not listen to them, *as the LORD had said.*" Exodus 9:35 (after the seventh sign) says, "The heart of Pharaoh was hardened, and he did not let the people of Israel go, *just as the LORD had spoken through Moses.*" Since Scripture itself indicates by these phrases that it is very important to demonstrate that these events unfold *just as God said they would,* how likely is it that the predictions that God had made might or might not have been fulfilled? If God intended his prophecies (like the ones stated in Exodus 3:19-20) to be conditional, do you think God would then call attention to the fact that they were happening *just as he had said?* This makes no sense, and I submit that to suggest otherwise is to pull out of the narrative exactly what God intentionally built into it, that God is *God* precisely (in part) because he declares what will come, and that when it comes to pass, Scripture calls to our attention to the fact that it has been accomplished *just as God said it would.* To understand this as conditional prophecy, then, is to undermine the very stated basis by which God himself proves his deity.

5. *Argument from supplementary predictions, equally remarkable, equally non-conditional.* The predictions of Exodus 3:19-20 do not stand alone. God predicts other things in this narrative, also utterly

remarkable, that also come about just as he said they would. Consider, for example, the very next verses: Exodus 3:21-22 records God's promise that he will grant the people favor in the eyes of the Egyptians so that when they leave, they will ask and be given gifts of gold and silver, and so will "plunder the Egyptians" (3:22). Incredible! Here, God predicts not just what one man (Pharaoh) will do, but what a whole nation of free persons will do. Are we to suppose that Israel should take this as a conditional prophecy? Absolutely nothing in the narrative would suggest that Israel (or we) are meant to understand this promise as conditional (unlike the Jonah example, where we do have compelling reason in the narrative itself to see it as a conditional prophecy).[10] And think how staggering this prediction is! Imagine how you would feel if you were an Egyptian going through plague after plague, while you noticed that the Israelites were being exempt from every one of them! How maddening! In fact, even before the plagues began, when the Egyptians placed on the Israelites an even greater burden (Exodus 5), we read that the Israelites said to Moses, "you have made us stink in the sight of Pharaoh and his servants, and have put a sword in their hand to kill us" (5:21). Even before the plagues, Israel was despised by Egypt. Then come nine plagues, and Egypt is nearly devastated. Yet we read in Exodus 11:1-3 and 12:35-36 that the Israelites (these slaves in Egypt) asked the Egyptians for their treasures and the Egyptians complied! And the only reason for this is given in the text: "The LORD had given the people favor in the sight of the Egyptians, so that they let them have what they asked. Thus they plundered the Egyptians" (12:36). Consider again these two passages: Exodus 3:21-22 (the prediction that Israel would be given favor and plunder the Egyptians) and Exodus 12:35-36 (the outcome, in which Israel was given favor, received the treasures of the Egyptians when they asked for them, and so plundered the Egyptians). Is it reasonable to think that the prediction in Exodus 3:21-22 was conditional? I find absolutely no reason to think so and massive reason to conclude that God predicted exactly what he knew a whole nation of free persons would do.

The proposal that the prediction of God to Moses in Exodus 3:19-20 was conditional, while initially intriguing as a general idea, is simply lacking merit as one considers this prediction in context. Rather, there is compelling biblical reason to see this as a prediction 1) of what God *knew* would occur, and 2) of things that involved the *future choices and actions of a free agent.* Therefore, this text conflicts at a fundamental level with the openness proposal; and it displays, contrary to open theism, God's knowledge of these future human choices and actions as evidence for his very deity as the one and only true God.

MEDITATION ON PSALM 139

What great comfort Psalm 139 gives to God's people as it extols God's intimate acquaintance with all our ways. Consider first the amazing claim of verse 4: "Even before a word is on my tongue, behold, O LORD, you know it altogether." How can one do justice to this text from the perspective that God does not know the future? When Psalm 139:4 declares that God *knows* the words we speak before we open our mouths, can this be reduced to God's *informed guesses* as to what we will say? If so, it simply is not true to say that God *knows* our words in advance. We all say surprising things, surprising sometimes even to ourselves. No amount of past and present knowledge of individuals could predict with complete accuracy the words they will speak next. But Psalm 139:4 declares that God *knows in advance* all the words we speak.

Furthermore, this declaration that God knows our every word before we utter it is merely an example of the general principle, stated in verses 1-5, that God knows and oversees every aspect of our lives. The God who knows when we sit and rise (v. 2), who understands our every thought (v. 2), who searches out our paths (v. 3), who hems us in behind and before (v. 5), is the God who also knows all our words before any is uttered. Meticulous providential oversight is depicted in ways that inspire in God's people great confidence that all of their lives are under his supervision. While we marvel that God knows precisely and exactly every word before we speak, this is just one example of how meticulous is God's care and oversight of our lives.

Verse 16 of this psalm provides another glimpse into the extent of God's meticulous oversight of his creatures: "Your eyes saw my unformed substance; in your book were written, every one of them, the days that were formed for me, when as yet there were none of them." Clearly this passage indicates that God "forms" or "ordains" the days of our lives before we even exist. But how can this be? How can God form all our days when (according to open theism) God does not know any of the multitude of the future contingencies and future free actions of ourselves and of other people that may relate to our lives? The fact is that without foreknowledge of a contingent future, God could not even know *that* we would be (e.g., God could not know what individuals might be miscarried or die in childbirth), much less *know the days* that would occupy our lives, and much less again *ordain* them all from the outset. Clearly we are intended to be comforted with the assurance that God knows *all that will happen to us.*

Consider this feature a bit further. For God to know all the days

47

of our lives when as yet there were none of them (v. 16), God must *know about* and be in *command of* all the contingencies and future free will choices that will happen in regard to our lives. To ordain the days of our lives is both to *know about* and to *have regulative power over* the host of innumerable variables that go into making the substance of each and every one of those days. Consider just one day. Take today, for example. Think about the multitude of variables that affect your life this day. You are living, but could you have died? Might you have been involved in a car accident? Did you get your exercise in, so that your good health will persist? How might your diet and level of stress affect your life, well-being, and longevity? How many other people made free decisions today that had potential impact on your life and well-being? *Consider all of this and much, much more just for one single day.* The fact is that God cannot be subject to and limited by the free choices of people over which he has no prior knowledge or regulative control and still be able to know and ordain all the days of our life.[11] The fact is, then, that Psalm 139:16 confronts us with a reality that simply cannot be accounted for in open theism. God knows our future days, all of them, from before there was one of them. No wonder the psalmist marvels and places unfailing confidence in this genuinely omniscient God.

MEDITATION ON DANIEL 11

The book of Daniel, with its series of highly specific and detailed predictive dreams, spanning the breadth of many centuries and involving the rise and fall of many nations, offers enormous data in support of God's exhaustive knowledge of all that will take place in the future. One cannot dismiss the predictions of chapters 2, 4, 5, 7, 8, 9, 10 and 11 by saying that God controls merely *a minimal select por-*

tion of the features of the future, sufficient to ensure that these predictions come true. A reasonable consideration of the details as well as the breadth involved renders such an accounting simplistic. Especially when one factors in the staggering number of future free will decisions that would have to line up just right for these events to come true, these chapters provide overwhelming evidence for God's comprehensive knowledge of and control over the future. In the limited space that can be devoted to Daniel's predictions, I will try to summarize what is involved predictively for just some of the detailed prophecies of *one* of these chapters.

Daniel 11 contains, by itself, an amazing array of instances in which God predicts, and hence foreknows, many future events and many future free creaturely actions. For example, Daniel, prophesying in the first year of Cyrus, king of Persia (ca. 539 B.C.), predicts three kings to come after Cyrus, followed by a fourth (v. 2). This fourth king, likely a reference to the coming Alexander the Great (reigned ca. 336–323), died young, and his sons were murdered. Daniel predicts this, along with the fact that his kingdom would be divided into four parts (v. 4). Amazingly, as history unfolds, Alexander's four generals vie for control and split the kingdom into the four regions of Egypt (south), Syria (north), Asia Minor, and Greece proper. The general of the south (Egypt), Ptolemy I, began the line of the Ptolemies, while Syria's king, Seleucus I, began the line of the Seleucids. Daniel 11:5-35 then describes predictively roughly 155 years of warfare between the Seleucids and Ptolemies, with special focus given to the despicable reign of Antiochus IV Epiphanes (vv. 21-35), an unrightful heir to the throne. All these events, the people who fulfill them, and many more details than here described, are predicted with amazing accuracy by Daniel.

Furthermore, it must not be missed that most, perhaps all, of the items prophesied required for their fulfillment enormous numbers of future free human choices and actions. God knew that three kings, then a fourth, would come to power. He knew the kingdom would be divided and that the four parts of it would be ruled by kings other than that fourth king's descendents. He knew of the battles that would take place between two of these powers, and of the ultimate victory of one. He knew of the devastation that would come to Israel through this last wicked king, and he knew this wicked king would not be the rightful heir to the throne. Each one of these predictions involves a multitude of future free human actions for it to occur. It is no wonder that liberals date this portion of Daniel very late! So many details, involving future free choices, with such precision—this is truly overwhelming evidence, in one chapter of the Bible, of the reality of God's foreknowledge.[12]

MEDITATION ON JOHN 13:19 AND 38

Several places in John we find Jesus appealing to his knowledge of the future so that others may believe "that I am he." Consider John 13:19: "I am telling you this now, before it takes place," Jesus tells his disciples, "that when it does take place you may believe that I am he" (cf. 14:29; 16:4). The point is the same as in Isaiah (remember John 12:37-41, where John identifies Jesus with the God of Isaiah's vision). Jesus' knowledge of the future is evidence that he has the knowledge of God.

In light of Jesus' claim in John 13:19, consider a few specific examples in John of Jesus' foreknowledge. We find Jesus telling Peter of his three denials before the rooster crows (see John 13:38 with 18:15-27); predicting the kind of death Peter would die (John 21:18-

19); and predicting that Judas would be the one to betray him (John 6:64, 70-71; cf. Matt. 26:21-25). In all of these cases, Jesus' predictions require that other humans do precisely what Jesus predicted they would do. Yet these predictions are not presented as mere guesses regarding the future. Rather, Jesus *knows* what other free agents will in fact choose to do, *states* what these future actions will be, and provides his *reason* for so doing: "that when it does take place you may believe that I am he."

Consider more fully Christ's remarkable prediction in John 13:38 that before the rooster crowed, Peter would deny him *three*—not one, or two, or four, or forty, but *three*—times. Greg Boyd has explained this remarkable prediction on the basis of Jesus' perfect knowledge (as revealed to him by the Father) of Peter's past conduct and character.[13] That is, because God (and so, Jesus) can know exactly what Peter is like, what he is inclined to do or not do, therefore, Christ was able to predict that Peter would deny Christ these three times. Is this a reasonable basis for explaining this account? Surely it is true that Jesus knew Peter's character, but how could he surmise *three denials* (i.e., precisely *this* future occurrence) from knowledge of Peter's character? Consider: What if Peter had become so frightened, shocked, bewildered, and confused after the first confrontation and denial that he decided to run off into the wilderness, thus making the second and third denials impossible? What if after the first or second denial those surrounding Peter had grabbed him and taken him before the chief counsel, where Peter denied Christ repeatedly and incessantly to avoid the torture he would otherwise receive, by this denying Christ a multitude of times, not merely three? What if James and John had gone with Peter to the fire where the denials occurred, but because of their presence with him, he found himself ashamed either to deny

Christ or to affirm him, and instead remained silent and then made some excuse in order to leave as hastily as possible? In the open view, since Jesus (or the Father) does not know the future free actions of people, he cannot have known whether any of these possible and reasonable scenarios (or innumerable others) might have occurred. The proposal that Jesus could accurately predict that *Peter would deny him precisely three times,* based on God's perfect knowledge of Peter's character is biblically and logically implausible.

Consider another feature of this case, namely, how many future free actions were involved in the fulfillment of this prediction. Clearly all of Peter's choices to deny Christ were his free choices. Those who questioned and confronted Peter also did so freely. That they confronted him three times was their free choice. That all three questions but no more occurred before the rooster crowed involved their free choice, for many factors may have led either to their delaying to ask Peter the questions they did until well after sunrise, or to asking several more questions in rapid succession, thus causing Peter to make more than three denials before the rooster crowed. That no harm befell Peter, preventing him from arriving at the fireside, involved both his and many others' free choices. That no other disciples were with Peter who might have strengthened his resolve not to deny Christ involved many people's freedom of choice. And on and on. Clearly, the only full and satisfying explanation of this prediction is that Jesus knew exactly that, how often, and when Peter would deny him. To deny foreknowledge here is to deny the obvious basis for this prediction, and is to rob Jesus of the grounding of his own claim to deity.

MEDITATION ON JOHN 18:4

Another specific example in which the openness understanding simply does not fit what we find in Scripture may be noticed in John 18:4.[14] It reads, "Then Jesus, knowing all that would happen to him, came forward and said to them, 'Whom do you seek?'" This passage is relevant to the central openness denial of exhaustive definite foreknowledge in at least two ways.

1. *Argument from Jesus' comprehensive claim to know all coming things.* The explicit claim of John (v. 4a) that Jesus knew "all that would happen to him" is astonishing in itself for its overt and explicit claim of comprehensive knowledge of these future events. Consider how many specific actions and events must comprise the "all" that Jesus is here said to know: the guards, the soldiers, the trials, the accusations, the questioning, the beatings, the denials, the betrayals, the release of Barabbas, the thorns, the cross. Just the sheer amount of factual knowledge about the future claimed in this statement defies explanation apart from God's having exhaustive foreknowledge. But consider, further, how many of these future actions and events occurred as they did, and occurred as Jesus knew they would, only by the free-choice decisions of numerous human moral agents. Every soldier's strike or false accusation or stated blasphemy or hurtful lie or mocking act of honor or hammer blow was done by some free will agent or another. According to open theism, God could know none of those future free will actions. But this text tells us differently; this text tells us that Jesus knew "all the things" that were coming upon him. In other words, this text tells us that Jesus knew what open theists say he could not know.

2. *Argument from Jesus' question to those seeking him.* The question Jesus asked those coming to arrest him (v. 4b) offers important

insight into how Scripture is rightly to be interpreted as it relates to open theism. Directly upon telling us that Jesus knew *all* that was coming upon him, John records Jesus as then, of all things, asking a question. How odd, one might think. Don't you ask questions when you *lack* knowledge? Isn't the purpose of asking a question to *gain* knowledge one does not currently possess? Normally, one might think this is so. But the juxtaposition of the question following immediately on the heels of John's claim that Jesus knew "all that would happen to him," shows that we would misinterpret the question were we to read it as a tacit admission of Jesus' lack of knowledge (say, for example, that he didn't know if they were seeking him alone, or him along with his disciples, or perhaps hoped that they were after some escaped criminal, or even that he was so distraught and confused that he did not know what was taking place). But as one reads on in the passage, it is clear just why Jesus *does* ask the question. He wants them to state clearly that they seek "Jesus of Nazareth" so that he can respond by claiming, "I am *he.*" Over and over in John, Jesus has made his claim to deity clear with the use (among other things) of "I am" applied to himself (John 8:58 being perhaps the most notable example). In light of the Gospel of John's regular use of "I am" in relation to Jesus' deity, and in light of the reaction of falling to the ground by those who heard him (18:6), it seems that Jesus is clearly doing more than simply identifying himself as this particular person. His assertion of deity is implicit. So, the question, far from indicating Jesus' lack of knowledge, is meant to bring forth his claim of boundless deity. As Ardel Caneday has commented, while Jesus' question *veiled* his deity to his rebellious listeners, his answer, ironically, *revealed* his deity.[15]

What can we learn from John 18:4 about how best to interpret some of the favorite "openness" passages? Simply put, God may have reasons for speaking to us or approaching us in ways that, *in and of themselves,* may seem to indicate that he lacks knowledge. Asking questions, certainly, may be one expression of such an apparent limitation of God's knowledge. But here we learn, by interpreting the question of 18:4b in light of the unambiguous assertion in 18:4a, that Jesus' question meant no such lack of knowledge. Instead, it was a tool to elicit from others what he wanted from them, to advance his own purposes in fulfilling his prior will. Openness proponents tell us often that they mean only to take the straightforward meaning of the Bible seriously. But does not this passage illustrate that a straightforward way of interpreting Jesus' question (i.e., as indicating, by implication, his limited knowledge) may in fact lead to a false interpretation (i.e., because John tells us explicitly that Jesus knew all things that would happen to him)? May it not be that God's intended meaning is far more complex and indirect than the openness hermeneutic of "literal," "straightforward," or "face-value" readings of passages would permit? And if so, is it not also clear that to take the "straightforward" meaning of the text in such cases as the intended meaning is, in fact, to *miss entirely what the intended meaning actually is?* Clearly this would be the case here: if we took Jesus' question in a straightforward fashion as indicating a limitation in his knowledge, this would not be a mere "alternate" interpretation of this passage; in fact, it would misinterpret the passage altogether and violate the explicit statement of John in the first half of the verse.

What is helpful about John 18:4 is that the "correction" to a potential misinterpretation of Jesus' question (v. 4b) is provided in the direct and explicit assertion of Christ's transcendent and comprehensive foreknowledge of these future events (v. 4a). This is not always the case, however. We do not always find in the very same verse (or immediate context) the "transcendent" truth that the alleged *straightforward* interpretation, indicating some apparent limitation in God's knowledge, cannot be the truly *intended* meaning of the passage. We must rather search the Scriptures as a whole and seek to interpret Scripture in light of Scripture, while also working hard at understanding each passage in its own context. When this is done, the transcendent truth of God's exhaustive foreknowledge will lead us to think harder and deeper about specific passages that appear to conflict. We will ask, Why did God choose to say it this way, in light of his clear teaching elsewhere that he knows all things? This is the path to exploring the truly intended meanings of these texts. The openness interpretive approach, for all its claim to take Bible passages seriously, commends an approach that actually violates those passages and diminishes the God of Scripture. John 18:4 helps us see that this is so.

CONCLUSION

Does Scripture teach that God wonders and guesses what free human persons might do in the future, as open theists say he does? Does he "get it wrong" sometimes, thinking, for example, that surely Saul will make a good king, but then regretting his own decision to make him king? Or, deciding to flood the world, but then considering that this choice might have been a bit too severe? Do we live life with a God who second-guesses his own actions, and who waits to find out if the counsel he has given to others will prove to be best, or true?

"Absolutely not," the church has said throughout its history. And once again, Christian people must arise and say no to this proposal.

The God of the Bible demonstrates the truthfulness of his own claim to deity by predicting the future with astonishing and mind-boggling precision. This foreknowledge of God encompasses both the immediate (the next word off my tongue) and the remote (what nations and kings will do centuries in the future). The God of the Bible does not face the future as we do—wondering what might happen. No, the true God knows and declares the end from the beginning, and he challenges anyone to prove him wrong!

Since passages cited in defense of the open view can rightly be explained differently than openness proponents insist, and since so much Scripture compels us to bow before the God who knows the sweep of history in its vast detail, we simply must see that the case for open theism from Scripture fails. Sadly, this is not the only aspect of the open view that is troubling. As this misunderstanding of Scripture and its teaching about God is then applied to life, issues like prayer and suffering and Christian hope are strained beyond recognition within a truly Christian context. We turn next, then, to look selectively at some of the ways in which this misguided view of Scripture leads to deep and troubling distortions for understanding and living the Christian life. In all of this, our hope and prayer is that we will see the true glory of God and be compelled to bow before his majestic greatness, and not be lured by a fashionable human-like deity that belittles both God and the faith he wishes to elicit in his people. For the greater glory of God, and the lasting good of God's people, then, we continue.

3

OPEN THEISM AND SUFFERING

CONTRASTING VISIONS

One of open theism's most forceful claims is that its view of God and his relationship with people allows us to account for suffering and affliction far better than in traditional views of God. All traditional views of God have in common the belief that God knows in advance everything that will happen in the future, and that he knows all of these future actions and events with exacting detail. Furthermore, this traditional vision of God and the world affirms that while God knows all the suffering and evil that will occur in the future, he also knows that good purposes are ultimately served through this evil—good purposes that could be realized only with the suffering and affliction that actually does come to pass. This has never meant for Christian theologians, through the centuries, that God is morally responsible for evil or is the "author of sin,"[1] although he clearly and certainly creates the world knowing in advance exactly everything that will happen, including every single atrocity and tragedy.

If any version of the traditional view is true, argues the open theist, then two things follow: 1) the future with its "foreknown" suffering cannot be avoided, since God knows in advance exactly what will happen and his knowledge (including his foreknowledge), by definition, cannot be mistaken; and 2) God intentionally brings it about that every single horrific instance of suffering that he knows in advance will occur, *does occur.* In other words, God is unavoidably responsible for bringing into existence each and every instance of evil, since he knew these things would occur in the "future" that he would bring into existence.

So, argues the openness proponent, if we are to understand the future as truly free, and if we are to absolve God from moral responsibility for creating a world that would include all of the suffering that it does include, then we must deny that God knows and can know the future free decisions and actions of his moral creatures. When suffering occurs, we can rest assured that God neither planned it, nor did he will it, nor did he know of it in advance, nor does he have some "secret" purpose behind it. Rather, the God of open theism wishes that suffering and affliction never did occur, and whenever it does, he feels badly for it and he is there, in the suffering, to provide strength and hope to those undergoing pain.

CONTRASTING STORIES

Perhaps it would help to consider two contrasting stories of suffering, each illustrating how Christian people might face similar kinds of tragic circumstances when seen, respectively, through the church's traditional and the new openness view of God.

An Account of God's Knowledge and Purposefulness in Affliction (the Traditional View)

The names of Scott and Janet Willis are known to many Christians across this country for their faith and hope in God in the midst of an unspeakably tragic circumstance. The following portion of their story is told by Eric Zorn, a writer for the *Chicago Tribune*:

> Reverend Duane [Scott] Willis of the Parkwood Baptist Church in Chicago's Mount Greenwood neighborhood always bowed his head in prayer with his family before they took a journey together—"asking that God would protect us and give us a great trip, a good time together and, of course, safety," he says.
>
> One November morning [November 8, 1994], Duane and Janet Willis and six of their nine children said such a prayer, then headed for Milwaukee in their Plymouth Voyager minivan to visit relatives. Along the interstate, the van ran over a scrap of metal that had fallen off a truck ahead of them. The metal punctured the Willis gas tank and kicked up sparks that ignited a terrible explosion. Five of the children—aged 6 weeks to 11 years—were instantly consumed by fire. The sixth, 13-year-old Ben, was burned critically.
>
> Janet and Duane Willis were not seriously injured. Looking upon the scene, Duane told Janet, "This is what God has prepared us for." As she followed the charred bodies of her children to the ambulance, Janet Willis recited from the 34th Psalm, a prayer the Parkwood congregation had been attempting to memorize: "I will bless the Lord at all times. His praise shall continually be in my mouth." That Psalm goes on to observe, "Many are the afflictions of the righteous."
>
> From their own hospital beds, the Willises prayed for their son Ben to recover. When he died the next morning they did not stop praying, nor did they stop praising God. "God knows all of history and time from its beginning to its end," said Duane Willis several months later. "What happened to us wasn't an accident. God is never taken by surprise. God had a purpose for it, probably many purposes. We don't understand God's agenda—as Isaiah says, 'His ways are not our ways.' We asked him for safety and it didn't turn out that way, but it's in the way God answers our prayers that we come to understand what God's will is."[2]

One of the surviving sons of Scott and Janet Willis has also written about what his parents and family have experienced. To fill in a bit more of the story, here is a portion of this gripping account by Toby Willis:

My dad opened the press conference [following the accident] by quoting a psalm from the Bible. "I will bless the Lord at all times; His praise shall continually be in my mouth" (Ps. 34:1). Why this psalm? Even in the midst of physical and emotional pain, he knew from reading the Word of God that he was to trust that God is good.

Upon finishing his prepared statement, he answered questions from reporters. They were kind and compassionate. However, as most intelligent people would do, they politely asked if he could shed light upon the ancient question, "Why do bad things happen to good people?"

It is hard enough to publicly praise God in times of pain and suffering. But is anyone able to reasonably explain the why? Do matters of faith fall outside the explanations of reason? With cameras rolling, my dad had to face the sincere questions of reality.

My dad had already stated that he knew "God had reasons . . . and that God was good." Indeed the Bible tells us that all things work together for good to those who love God (Rom. 8:28). It also gives examples of people of the past, showing how God changed what appeared to be tragedy into good. The best example is the story of Joseph, recorded in the book of Genesis. In our limited knowledge of the past and present and our inability to see the future, we simply do not yet see the finished story. . . . Understanding how God views us, and the punishment we deserve, my dad correctly remarked to the reporter that "the question should really be changed to, why do good things happen to bad people?"[3]

One cannot help but see the confidence in God and his wise and good character pervading these reports. Scott and Janet Willis had a confidence in God that led them to rejoice in him, even as their children were being taken from them by the Lord. Another report of this tragedy records Scott saying, regarding his precious children:

> We understood that they were given of the Lord, and we understood they weren't ours. They were His, and we were stewards of those children. And so God took them back. He is the Giver and Taker of life. We must tell you that we hurt and sorrow as you parents would for your children. The depth of pain is indescribable. The Bible expresses our feelings that we sorrow, but not as those without hope.[4]

The themes of God's knowledge of all that happens, his ultimate good purposes in the midst of tragedy, the confidence that nothing takes God by surprise, and the assurance that our lives are in his hands—these themes exude from the lives and lips of Scott and Janet Willis. For them, God knows all that occurs, works in all things to accomplish his good yet mysterious purposes, and can be counted on to do what is best even when it involves our deep sorrow and pain. Recall again Scott Willis's words, "What happened to us wasn't an accident. God is never taken by surprise. God had a purpose for it, probably many purposes."

An Account of God's Ignorance and Purposelessness in Affliction (the Openness View)

In striking contrast to this account stands one offered by Greg Boyd. He tells of being approached by an angry young woman after having preached a sermon on how God directs our paths.[5] In brief, this woman (whom he calls 'Suzanne') was a committed Christian single with a zeal for missions. She prayed fervently for God to bring to her a missions-minded young man who shared her burden, in particular, for Taiwan. In college, she met such a man, spent rich times of prayer and fellowship together with him over three-and-a-half years, and after a prolonged period of seeking God's will—including a lengthy period of fasting and seeking much godly counsel—they married, fully confident that God had brought them together. Following college, and two years into their missionary training, Suzanne learned that her husband was involved in an adulterous relationship. He repented (or so it appeared), but several months later he returned to his involvement in this affair, began treating Suzanne very badly, and eventually divorced her to move in with his lover. Within weeks of the divorce, Suzanne learned that she was pregnant (with his child, of course), leaving her, now at the end of this horrible ordeal, emotionally and spiritually empty. Boyd writes,

> Understandably, Suzanne could not fathom how the Lord could respond to her lifelong prayers by setting her up with a man he *knew* would do this to her and her child. Some Christian friends had suggested that perhaps she hadn't heard God correctly. But if it wasn't God's voice that she and everyone else had heard regarding this marriage, she concluded, then no one could ever be sure they heard God's voice.[6]

Confronted with this agonizing situation, and seeking to help this hurting and angry woman deal with her pain, loss, and sense of divine betrayal, Boyd explains the pastoral counsel he offered to her:

> Initially, I tried to help Suzanne understand that this was her ex-husband's fault, not God's, but her reply was more than adequate

to invalidate my encouragement: If God *knew* exactly what her husband would do, then he bears all the responsibility for setting her up the way he did. I could not argue against her point, but I could offer an alternative way of understanding the situation.

I suggested to her that God felt as much regret over the confirmation he had given Suzanne as he did about his decision to make Saul king of Israel (1 Sam. 15:11, 35; see also Gen. 6:5-6). Not that it was a bad decision—at the time, her ex-husband was a good man with a godly character. The prospects that he and Suzanne would have a happy marriage and fruitful ministry were, at the time, very good. Indeed, I strongly suspect that he had influenced Suzanne and her ex-husband toward this college with their marriage in mind.

Because her ex-husband was a free agent, however, even the best decisions can have sad results. Over time, and through a series of choices, Suzanne's ex-husband had opened himself up to the enemy's influence and became involved in an immoral relationship. Initially, all was not lost, and God and others tried to restore him, but he chose to resist the prompting of the Spirit, and consequently his heart grew darker. Suzanne's ex-husband had become a very different person from the man God had confirmed to Suzanne to be a good candidate for marriage. This, I assured Suzanne, grieved God's heart at least as deeply as it grieved hers.

By framing the ordeal within the context of an open future, Suzanne was able to understand the tragedy of her life in a new way. She didn't have to abandon all confidence in her ability to hear God and didn't have to accept that somehow God intended this ordeal "for her own good." Her faith in God's character and her love toward God were eventually restored and she was finally able to move on with her life. . . . This isn't a testimony to his [God's] exhaustive definite foreknowledge; it's a testimony to his unfathomable wisdom.[7]

As John Sanders explains, while God gives people freedom to be used for good purposes, he does not intend for it to be used for evil, and he has no hidden "good purpose" for specific instances of suffering that occur. Sanders would agree with Boyd that we should reject the notion that somehow God intends suffering in our lives "for our own good." God neither knows in advance that affliction will happen nor wills it to occur. When it does happen, suffering and pain serves no divine purpose, and we should not "dignify" such suffering and evil by saying that somehow God intends it for good. Putting this understanding within his larger view of God's relationship to the world, Sanders explains:

> The overarching structures of creation are purposed by God, but not every single detail that occurs within them. Within general providence it makes sense to say that God intends an overall purpose for the creation and that God does not specifically intend each and every action within the creation. Thus God does not have a specific divine purpose for each and every occurrence of evil. The "greater good" of establishing the conditions of fellowship between God and creatures does not mean that gratuitous evil has a point. Rather, the possibility of gratuitous evil has a point but its actuality does not. . . . When a two-month-old child contracts a painful, incurable bone cancer that means suffering and death, it is pointless evil. The Holocaust is pointless evil. The rape and dismemberment of a young girl is pointless evil. The accident that caused the death of my brother was a tragedy. God does not have a specific purpose in mind for these occurrences.[8]

These stories reveal two very different approaches to the question of human suffering. In the traditional view of God, God knows all that will occur, including all suffering, and he creates the world knowing both that the suffering will occur and that his good purposes will be accomplished through it. In the open view, this simply is not the case. Rather, the God of open theism does not know, intend, or will good out of any future suffering. Perhaps it would be helpful to list some of the main beliefs that go into the open view's understanding of suffering and pain. According to open theism:

1. God does not know in advance the future free actions of his moral creatures.
2. God cannot control the future free actions of his moral creatures.
3. Tragic events occur over which God has no control (because of the way he has designed the world to be).
4. When such tragedies occur, God should not be blamed, because he was not able to prevent them from occurring (because of the way he has designed the world to be), and he certainly did not will or cause them to occur.
5. When such tragic events occur, God feels the pain of those who endure suffering.
6. God is love, and he may be trusted always to do his best to offer guidance that is intended to serve the well-being of others.
7. At times, God realizes that the guidance he gave may have inadvertently and unexpectedly led to unwanted hardship and suffering.
8. At times, God may repent of his own past actions, realizing that his own choices have not worked out well and may have led to unexpected hardship (e.g., 1 Sam. 15:11).

9. Suffering is gratuitous and pointless, i.e., suffering has no positive or redeeming quality to it at all, so that God should never be seen as intending suffering in order to bring some good from it.

10. Regardless of whether our suffering was pointless, or whether God may have contributed inadvertently to our suffering, God always stands ready to help rebuild our lives and offers us further grace, strength, direction, and counsel.

UNDERSTANDING SUFFERING BIBLICALLY

Because Scripture is the only final and fully authoritative source for Christian faith and practice, the most critical question we can ask is, Does the open view of suffering reflect accurately what Scripture teaches? While much more could be said, this brief summary will be sufficient to show that many of Scripture's central teachings regarding suffering simply cannot be accounted for in the open view, and because of this, Christian faith and hope in God will be harmed where open theism is followed. Please consider these biblical principles:

1. Suffering is not, in itself, an *essential* good. On this point, open theists and traditional theists agree. Scripture is absolutely clear: God is good and *only* good! Psalm 5:4 affirms, "For you are not a God who delights in wickedness; evil may not dwell with you" (cf. Ps. 11:5-7; 92:15); and Psalm 107:1 exhorts, "Oh give thanks to the LORD, for he is good, for his steadfast love endures forever!" (cf. Ps. 100:5; 106:1; 136:1). Scripture is equally clear that the creation God made was, like God, good and *only* good. "And God saw everything that he had made, and behold, it was very good" (Gen. 1:31). It is also clear

that in God's future re-creation that we call heaven, all evil, suffering, and pain will be done away entirely. Revelation 21:3-4 states, "And I heard a loud voice from the throne saying, 'Behold, the dwelling place of God is with man. He will dwell with them, and they will be his people, and God himself will be with them as their God. He will wipe away every tear from their eyes, and death shall be no more, neither shall there be mourning nor crying nor pain anymore, for the former things have passed away'" (cf. Rev. 22:1-5). We must affirm, then, that evil can have no place either in the very nature of God or in the created order as God created it, or in the heaven God will re-create. Suffering, then, is not essential to the nature of God or of creation as made by God.

2. But suffering is often ordained by God, and intentionally used by God, as an *instrumental* good. That is, although suffering is not good in itself, it can and does sometimes serve good purposes, as an instrument in God's hand. These good purposes often stand behind suffering as part of God's design for people. Clearly, this is a crucial point where open theists depart from church tradition on the question of suffering. Whereas open theists claim that suffering is not designed by God and has no intended good purpose behind it, orthodox Christians have held over the centuries that in fact God does design at least some suffering for the express purpose of bringing about some good through it.

Consider some examples from Scripture where we see God employing pain and affliction as his instruments for good. First, suffering can sometimes be God's designed and appointed means of divine judgment over those who are opposed to him, even bringing them to death if their hardness of heart continues (e.g., Num. 16:31-35, 41-50; Isa. 10:5-19). Second, similarly, God designs some pain to function as his tool of discipline to call wayward children back to him (e.g., Prov. 3:12; Heb. 12:10). As C. S. Lewis has said, pain is God's "megaphone" calling to rebellious hearts.[9] Third, affliction can be appointed by God for the growth and strengthening of believers' faith (e.g., Rom. 5:3-5; James 1:2-4). Fourth, affliction can expose human weakness so that the surpassing strength and glory of God may be more evident (e.g., 2 Cor. 4:8-12; 12:8-10). Fifth, affliction can be given by God so that believers will be better able to minister to others who, likewise, experience pain and suffering in their lives (e.g., 2 Cor. 1:3-7). Sixth, suffering is simply a necessary part of one's discipleship to Christ, in that following the path Christ walked will bring with it suffering to prove and test our allegiance to, and hope in, him alone (e.g., John 15:18-20; Phil. 3:10; 2 Tim. 3:12).

3. In particular, God has promised his children that nothing befalls their lives that is not ordered and used by him for their ultimate good. Romans 8:28 offers a promise so precious, so comforting, it is unimaginable that one could deny this and still affirm the Christian faith: "And we know that for those who love God all things work together for good, for those who are called according to his purpose." So when Sanders says, "God does not have a specific purpose in mind for these [tragic] occurrences,"[10] and when Boyd asserts regarding the betrayal Suzanne experienced, "She didn't have to abandon all confidence in her ability to hear God and didn't have to accept that somehow God intended this ordeal 'for her own good,'"[11] this counsel by open theists strips from Christians the very hope and confidence in God that Scripture intends them to have. Over and over, throughout the pages of Scripture, whether through the story of Job or Joseph or David or Daniel or Jesus or Paul or Peter or so many, many more—throughout the Bible, the message is clear: God

orchestrates and uses suffering in the lives of his children for the purpose of bringing to them some ultimate (and at times immediate) good. God *does* intend good purposes through suffering, and Christians are robbed of this precious confidence by the open view's denial of this cherished truth.

Recently I spoke at a conference in which we thought at some length about how Christians should understand and face suffering. During the Q & A time, one sincere Christian woman asked, "I know that we are supposed to give thanks *in* everything that comes our way, but we're not expected to give thanks *for* everything, are we?" Well, the truth is, we are. Scripture commands both—thanks *in* and thanks *for* all that comes into our lives (see 1 Thess. 5:18 and Eph. 5:20, respectively). And of course this only makes sense. If the suffering that comes into our lives is pointless, if God has no good intent for it, and if all that it does is cause harm, then there is no reason to give thanks *in* the suffering, and certainly not *for* the suffering. You cannot genuinely give thanks in the suffering if you think that there is simply nothing about this that can possibly be a basis for giving thanks, that God is not in it (that in fact he feels badly about it and wishes it weren't happening), that Satan is chuckling over this, knowing that it serves no good purpose and only will bring harm, and that there is no assurance that the suffering will end any differently than it began—pointless, meaningless, and void of any and all possible good purpose. If that is how we think of suffering, we can only (rightly) despair *in* it and *for* it.

But if the promises of God are sure; if God has promised that he will ensure that *all things* will work together for good (Rom. 8:28); if God has promised that "those who seek the LORD lack no good thing" (Ps. 34:10; cf. Ps. 84:11); and if God wishes us to embrace his loving commitment to us as demonstrated when he says, "He who did not spare his own Son but gave him up for us all, how will he not also with him graciously give us all things?" (Rom. 8:32); then we have good reason to give God thanks both *in* and *for* all that occurs. God will not fail; he reigns over the suffering of our lives, and he purposes our good through everything that happens, ensuring that all the good he intends for us to have, we will have. What hope, what confidence, what peace, what joy, and what strength, all in the midst of suffering, that God wants his people to have.

4. God is more concerned with our character than with our comfort, with our transformation than with the trials necessary to get us where he wants us to be. Two passages sing this truth with echoes that sound something like the "Hallelujah Chorus." James has the audacity (so it would seem) to say to suffering and persecuted Christians, "Count it all joy, my brothers, when you meet trials of various kinds, for you know that the testing of your faith produces steadfastness. And let steadfastness have its full effect, that you may be perfect and complete, lacking in nothing" (James 1:2-4). Is it not clear that the openness understanding of suffering simply cannot account for this text? Indeed, for followers of the God of open theism, when suffering occurs, we grieve and God grieves with us, but we have no reason for rejoicing, for God is not in it and intends no good purpose through it. How can open theism affirm what is here commanded by James?

But Christians through the centuries have understood exactly why James instructs them to "count it all joy" when suffering and trials come. God's good hand is not absent, but present, in and through the suffering, so that we can believe and hold onto our confidence that God will use the suffering we experience for the strengthening of our faith. Far from viewing trials as the purposeless byproducts of living in a world where forces of nature run amok, or where wicked free creatures have their way in attempting to ruin our lives, rather, we are instructed to see the wise and good hand of God in all the trials of life, and so we have hope.

Similarly, Paul enjoins us believers to "rejoice in our sufferings, knowing that suffering produces endurance, and endurance produces character, and character produces hope, and hope does not put us to shame, because God's love has been poured into our hearts through the Holy Spirit who has been given to us" (Rom. 5:3-5). The only possible way that believers can rejoice and not despair in the face of suffering is if the good hand of God is in those very sufferings. Take away the providential hand of God, take away the good purpose served by the suffering, take away the character formation, hope, and holiness that stand behind the suffering, and you take away all reason to rejoice. Only because God intends good through suffering can Christians live their lives as Scripture commands, and as countless numbers of Christians have lived over the centuries. Because God cares most deeply about our conformity to the very character of Christ as his holy people (see Eph. 1:4 and Rom. 8:29), and because God has deemed it wise and good to enlist suffering as one of his tools to bring about this good and perfect goal, we too can rejoice in our sufferings—not that the sufferings in themselves are good, but that they have a built-in purpose that is good. Apart from this good purpose, there is no hope.

5. Accepting the divine purpose for suffering does not require a passive acquiescence to suffering. Christians who believe that God's good purposes are fulfilled through suffering also realize that suffering *in itself* is not a good and so deliverance from it may rightly be

sought. Yet, while rightly seeking deliverance from suffering, Christians must also be ready to accept and embrace the possibility that God's best for us may include our continuing experience of the very suffering from which we correctly and passionately pray to be delivered. Paul's own experience is instructive. You'll recall Paul's description of his struggle with affliction (2 Cor. 12:7-10):

> So to keep me from being too elated by the surpassing greatness of the revelations [described in 12:1-6], a thorn was given me in the flesh, a messenger of Satan to harass me, to keep me from being too elated. Three times I pleaded with the Lord about this, that it should leave me. But he said to me, "My grace is sufficient for you, for my power is made perfect in weakness." Therefore I will boast all the more gladly of my weaknesses, so that the power of Christ may rest upon me. For the sake of Christ, then, I am content with weaknesses, insults, hardships, persecutions, and calamities. For when I am weak, then I am strong.

The same Paul who admonished believers to "rejoice in our sufferings" (Rom. 5:3) here, amid what must have been agonizing affliction, seeks God fervently to be released from the suffering he is undergoing. Is this an inconsistency? Not at all. For Paul knows that suffering is not a good thing in itself; its only "good" comes in what we learn through it, or how we grow because of it. So Paul pleads in prayer three times that God would take the affliction from him. But when it becomes clear to him that this thorn in the flesh, sent by Satan, was actually God's ordained tool to accomplish in Paul the work that this alone could do, Paul was able, then and only then, to accept the suffering as part of God's good purpose in his life.

Notice, too, the instructive tension between Paul seeing this affliction as a messenger from *Satan* and his praying to the *Lord* to remove it. If the thorn were only from Satan, it might seem that open theists are right to claim that God has nothing to do with evil. But surely this was not Paul's perspective at all. Amid his suffering, Paul did not initially look to God for comfort. On the contrary, he asked God to *remove* the affliction, believing that God had full power and authority over this affliction and could remove it if he wished. Ultimately, then, while this affliction came directly from Satan to harm Paul, indirectly and ultimately this affliction was permitted by the active agency and sovereign ordination of God, who could allow it to be given, could remove it when and if he wished, and would ordain that Paul experience it only if it served the good purposes that he (God), not Satan, had designed it to bring.

It is only in light of Paul's confidence that God's hand, ultimately, is behind his present experience of affliction that he can generalize for us what he has learned from his experience: "Therefore I will boast all the more gladly of my weaknesses, so that the power of Christ may rest upon me. For the sake of Christ, then, I am content with weaknesses, insults, hardships, persecutions, and calamities. For when I am weak, then I am strong" (2 Cor. 12:9b-10). His movement from this singular "thorn" of affliction to saying that he will boast gladly of his weaknesses (plural), and be content with weaknesses, insults, hardships, persecutions, and calamities (all plural), indicates his view that all such experiences are, similarly, under the oversight and providential guidance of God. Believers may have the hope that when they seek God earnestly and humbly, and when God says no to their prayers for deliverance, he does so for their good. Such confidence alone can account for the boasting and contentment in weaknesses that Paul urges. Never doubt, he would say to us, that God is in the affliction, that God is for us, and that his good purposes are accomplished through what he has willed that we should experience.

One final principle should be observed. Notice that Paul prayed *three times* for deliverance from this affliction. Not that "three" is magical; that's not the point. Rather, praying three times, instead of only once, indicates persistence in prayer. But praying three times, instead of endless prayers for deliverance, indicates Paul's willingness to accept "No" as God's answer to his pleading for relief. Paul prayed with persistence and perseverance, demonstrating his longing for God to grant what he sought, but then Paul assessed the reality of his ongoing affliction and came to see that God would not deliver him as he had hoped. At this point, Paul's whole disposition toward that unwelcome trial changed. Previously, he had viewed it as unwanted and hurtful. Now, seeing the good hand of God in ordaining that he have it, the trial became something of a gift from God's love for him. Clearly, Paul's prayer to *escape* the suffering had now changed to a longing to *embrace* that very suffering. And mind you, this was no mere acceptance of the inevitability of this affliction. Rather, the "boasting" and "contentment" in this and other afflictions indicate that Paul now saw his weakness more for the good that it would accomplish than for the hardship that it continued to bring him. Such is the wonder of knowing that God's good hand stands behind, and not apart from, the suffering that comes into our lives.

OTHER PROBLEMS WITH THE OPENNESS ACCOUNT OF SUFFERING

For all the celebration of open theism's ability better to deal with questions of suffering and affliction, it should be clear that Scripture stubbornly resists the open view on this issue. Yes, suffering is not in itself an essential good. But no, God is not absent from suffering, nor is suffering pointless. To the contrary, the believer's only sure hope and confidence in suffering is that God is very much involved in the affliction to bring about both what he has ordained by it and what is good for his child. On Scriptural grounds, then, open theism fails as a viable explanation for the existence of suffering and pain.

In addition, however, we should consider just what we would be left with if we were to adopt the open view of suffering. Does the open view actually absolve God from responsibility for suffering, as it claims to do? Does the open view give the believer the basis for more confidence in God? Consider a few problems that open theism faces.

1. It is hard to see that the God of open theism is as absent and removed from the outworking of human suffering and pain as open theists want us to envision. After all, even if suffering does occur, as proposed in open theism, by the misuse of creaturely freedom, so that free moral agents carry out hurtful and harmful actions, we still must ask, Does God know what is happening? And is he in a position where he could do something about it?

It simply won't do, it seems to me, to say that God is not involved when evil things happen to people, or that God has no intentions involved in relation to those evil occurrences. Why? Simply because, although God (as understood in open theism) does not and cannot know what free creatures will do with their future free choices, still, God knows everything past and present.

Consider a murder, for example. While the openness God does not and cannot know the future free action by which a murder will take place, he does fully know the character of the would-be murderer. He knows all of his thoughts, plans, meditations, discussions, motives, and intentions. And further, he sees perfectly as each situation (in the present) unfolds. Given this, would not God be in an ideal position to anticipate the likelihood of the murder occurring? Would not God observe the plot of the murder unfolding in exact detail (e.g., the man packing the weapon he plans to use, driving to the location where he intends to commit the murder, mulling over his strategy)?

Here is one place where the open view fails profoundly. Proponents of open theism want us to think that God is uninvolved in the suffering we experience, he feels as badly about it as we do, and there certainly is no divine purpose served by the evil. But the fact is, the open God was actively observing everything leading up to the point when the evil action or event transpired. He saw the whole thing develop, anticipated what would come, knew every relevant detail about it prior to the exact moment when it happened. Yet, knowing this, he did nothing—and he *chose* to do nothing. It simply is not true that God is uninvolved in the suffering we experience. God is very much involved, specifically allowing what he could easily prevent. The major difference between orthodox and openness views comes in answering this question: Is there divine purpose in the evil that happens? On the openness account, God specifically permits what he could prevent, knowing that it serves no good purpose. Orthodox accounts of God's relation to evil insist that, whether by the advantage given him by his exhaustive definite foreknowledge, or by his sovereign control over all of history, the God of historic Christianity specifically permits what he knows will ultimately serve some greater purpose. Suffering is not pointless, in that God can see just what purpose is served by all the suffering that occurs. God's knowledge of the future, because it is exhaustive and perfectly formed, grants him a view of history from its end. He can tell what purposes are fulfilled through suffering, and so believers can have confidence that God oversees the unfolding of history to ensure that it fulfills the good he intends in it.

The God of open theism is not absent from suffering, as proposed. Rather, he is very much present with almighty power to step in, but he chooses not to. Further, his specific permission of all suffering comes with this cost to Christian faith: he permits what he knows has no purpose and serves no good. How can it be better for Christian people to trust such a God? In fact, what trust is possible here? God's passivity toward suffering, not only allowing it (the orthodox view) but allowing it while not knowing whether it will be for our good or for our harm, leads not to hope but to despair, not to faith but to doubt, not to confidence but to dread. Clearly, this is neither the God of the Bible nor the God of true and vibrant Christian faith.

2. Recall the story of Suzanne, as told by Boyd, and consider this question: How can the God who, by his ignorance of the future, may lead you unwittingly into unanticipated and harmful suffering—how can this God now be your source of strength, comfort, and future leading? Boyd tells us that Suzanne was freed up to trust God, knowing that when God led her to marry the husband who proved to be unfaithful and hurtful, God didn't know this man would turn out this way. But surely an openness interpretation of this account will lead Christian people to turn *from* God rather than to trust him with yet more of their lives, with yet another major decision.

I have been in two public forums with Dr. Boyd, discussing these issues. In both forums (separated by more than a year) I have asked him the same question: Why should Suzanne think that God will do any better with guidance for her life in the future than he has done in the past? In neither setting was he able to give an answer. The fact is, the openness God has had several millennia of experience in dealing with human beings and their problems. Suzanne's experience has just recently happened, and it would seem that God still is not very capable of giving good leading, even after all this time. Just how often, throughout history, would stories like Suzanne's have occurred? How often has God looked back at his own well-intentioned advice and thought to himself, *If only I had known . . . . ?* And if this is the case, then what inspires us to place our lives, our confidence, our hope, our faith, our futures in the hands of this proposed God?

By its appeal to God's ignorance of the future, the openness solution to the problem of human suffering demeans and belittles God. This God becomes a sort of pathetic being, who tries so hard to lead his sincere children in ways that he hopes will be for their best, but instead, time and again, must watch helplessly as, in ways unknown to him, they are led into misery and suffering. We humans face this limitation when we give counsel to others; we just don't know for sure if taking that job or making this move or speaking with that person will turn out best. Now, we are told, God has the same problem. This can lead to only one conclusion: The God of open theism is just too small. This is not the God of the Bible, and this is not the God of Christian confidence, hope, faith, and joy.

3. Oddly and ironically, the God of open theism proves to be very impersonal, distant, and remote to believers during times of suffering. As one analyzes the picture of God and suffering portrayed in open theism, one sees a God who stands aloof—he cannot stop the suffering from happening, due to his previous purpose to let free creatures do as they wish with their freedom; and he cannot give

accurate counsel to those who are undergoing suffering, since he doesn't really know what the future holds. Further, he has no divine purpose served through the suffering and he only wishes that it were not happening. He sees no good that it will bring but he is helpless (by his own design) to do anything about it.

So, as believers face suffering with the God of open theism, they may wonder, *Where is God in all of this?* The only comfort that can be given is this: God is not here! He's not involved in the suffering, he has not willed it, he does not want it, he wishes it were not happening, and he won't do anything about it. For all intents and purposes, the God of open theism is an absentee deity during times of suffering, during the times when believers need most to know that God is with them, for them, and is working out his good and wise purposes amid the affliction that they endure.

This view of God has more in common with deism than with vital, vibrant, faith-filled Christianity. In deism, God creates the world and then lets things run in accordance with its built-in laws. In open theism, God creates the world with its bestowing of freedom to moral creatures, and he lets those creatures use their freedom, seldom interfering in what they do lest his plan and purpose to grant this freedom is shown to be a sham. In effect, the God of open theism watches helplessly as choices are made and actions are performed, often wishing things were different but uninvolved in those evil actions and unable to bring good out of them. This remote God, this distant God, this absentee God is not the God of the Bible.

Hear the words of Isaiah 43:1-2, expressing the promise of God's presence with his people amid their affliction: "But now thus says the LORD, he who created you, O Jacob, he who formed you, O Israel: 'Fear not, for I have redeemed you; I have called you by name, you are mine. When you pass through the waters, I will be with you; and through the rivers, they shall not overwhelm you; when you walk through fire you shall not be burned, and the flame shall not consume you.'" Please be clear that these words are not meant by God to ensure the absence of harm to God's people, for too many other places in Scripture indicate that God's people will suffer in their obedience to him (see, for example, the experiences of some of the faithful in Hebrews 11:36-38, who are mocked, flogged, imprisoned, stoned, and sawn in two precisely because of their faithfulness to God in a wicked and God-despising world). But Isaiah 43:1-2 does assure this: God's presence with his people amid their affliction guarantees that nothing can befall them that has not been "screened" by the wise, powerful, and providential hand of God. God is active and involved in their suffering, and his purposes are being worked out in and through it. God's children may have the confidence to know that God is for them, with them, and working to bring about what is best. But this is exactly the confidence robbed from Christian people in the open view of God. The God of the Bible knows all that will occur and therefore knows the good purposes that our trials and tribulations bring. Because the openness God can know neither of these things, and stands aloof watching helplessly during our suffering, this is not the God of Christian confidence nor the God of vibrant faith. Again, it is so clear, that their God is just too small.

A CONCLUDING STORY

Can anything be clearer from Scripture than this: the God of the Bible, the true and living God, wants and commands his people to put their hope entirely in him. Because he alone is infinitely wise, because he alone knows everything pertaining to our lives and the history and future of this world he has made, because he alone possesses indomitable power, because his ways are good and upright—for these and many more reasons, God insists that his people put their hope in him. But can Christian people really trust the God of open theism?

In January 1993, one moment's accident in our home resulted in months of deep anguish for our family and for our younger daughter in particular. I was at Trinity Evangelical Divinity School teaching an evening class, and my wife, Jodi, was at home with our two daughters, Bethany and Rachel (9 and 5 years old at the time), fixing dinner. Macaroni and cheese was on the menu this particular evening ("little bears," as Rachel still recalls). While both of our girls have loved to be near their mom while she worked around the house, Rachel in particular loved to "help Mommy" in the kitchen. Jodi had given Rachel some little kitchen assignments that she had finished, when she decided to "help" with the macaroni on the stove. Just moments previously, the water had come to a full boil, and Jodi had poured the box of dry macaroni into the pot. Within these couple moments, the water had resumed its full boil, when Rachel walked over to the stove, reached up from her short stature, grabbed the spoon, and attempted to give the macaroni a good stirring. Because of her position from below the pot, as Rachel proceeded to stir the macaroni, the pot shifted abruptly on the stove top, and much of the boiling macaroni and water sloshed out of the pot and landed directly on Rachel's left side—her left wrist and upper arm, her left leg, and one foot, all received a direct hit of boiling water. Jodi, who had been around the corner when this happened, heard Rachel scream. With Bethany's help, they rinsed the wounds with cool water and Jodi called emergency.

THEIR GOD IS TOO SMALL

They rushed to the only critical care unit open in the remote area of northern Illinois where we lived, and Rachel was treated for second- and third-degree burns. Jodi was instructed to call the hospital, where Rachel would need to be scheduled for daily "scrubbings" of the burned areas followed by fresh applications of a medicated cream and bandages. This began about a two-month process of taking Rachel for these daily bathings, scrubbings, and wrappings. A nurse would soak Rachel in an antiseptic bath for about thirty minutes, then, very gently but firmly, she would take a brush and scrub away dead flesh and skin from her tender little arm (which got the worst from the boiling water), and then rewrap the wounded areas with fresh Silvadene and bandages. I recall times in the car on the way to these treatments singing hymns with Rachel and Jodi and Bethany. Rachel's little heart was so tender to the Lord, and this experience only served to draw her closer. We would pray, and she would express her trust in God and pray that the Lord would bring healing to her body. Throughout this ordeal I talked with her of God's good and wise hand that both purposely allowed this to happen and surely would bring good through it. I witnessed in the life of this precious five-year-old daughter of mine such courage, strength, and faith as I have seldom witnessed in my life. Not once while driving to receive her "treatments"—knowing the pain that awaited her, with the scrubbing in particular—did Rachel complain. Most days, she was cheerful, singing, and we prayed much in the car on those trips. At this young age, with this experience of affliction, Rachel had unquestioning confidence in her God.

Now, I ask you, what if the God Rachel knew and prayed to had been the God of open theism? How would her story have been different? Well, here's what Rachel would have needed to know from the very first instant: "Rachel, God had *nothing* to do with this tragic accident of spilled boiling water. Yes, he was watching as you walked over to the stove and took the spoon in hand. Yes, he could see by your posture that you would have difficulty reaching high enough to stir the macaroni without spilling the water. Yes, he saw that the pot was very full of boiling water and that it wouldn't take much for it to tip and slosh a large quantity directly toward you. Yes, he could have intervened somehow—merely securing the pot in place as you stirred, so that it wouldn't shift and spill the water on you, would have been an 'easy' miracle to pull off. But no, he did not intervene to prevent this accident from happening, although he could have. And no, he did not allow it to happen because it would serve some good purpose. No, Rachel, God *did not* want this to happen, and it served *no good purpose* in his mind. In fact, Rachel, from God's perspective, this is just one more example of *totally pointless evil* about which he grieves, along with you, amid a multitude of tragic events he watches daily and wishes he could change. He just let the boiling water slosh out because in the world he made, lots of things 'just happen' that he wishes didn't happen and that he cannot control, since he has agreed basically to keep 'hands off.' So, Rachel, know this: God grieved as he watched your accident unfold and he feels as badly about it as you do. But you must know that God had absolutely nothing to do with it—laws of nature, in this case, were at work, and God simply cannot 'micro-manage' the world or it makes a mockery of how he has set things up. And furthermore, do not look for some reason or purpose God had in and through this. There isn't any. This is pointless suffering, period. And further yet, Rachel, please know that this sort of thing, or much worse, could very well happen again (and again and again) in the future, because God doesn't exercise any control over anything that happens and he certainly cannot know what sort of horrible and pointless tragadies may befall you. But now, Rachel, put your hope, and confidence, and faith, and life, in the hands of this God!"

The pathetic God of open theism results in a pathetic faith in his followers, and how we face suffering shows this more clearly than perhaps any other area of life. The God of the Bible commands our confidence, but the God of open theism leaves us fearful. The God of the Bible enlists our faith and hope as we face the future, but the God of open theism elicits fear and dread in the face of a future uncertain both to us and to God. The God of the Bible gives us a deep and profound sense of purpose in all the afflictions, sufferings, trials, and tribulations that we face, but the God of open theism tells us that all of our pain is pointless. The God of the Bible purposely allows all that happens, knowing exactly what he is doing and what purpose the suffering will accomplish, but the God of open theism strips both God and us of any and all hope in suffering. The God of the Bible truly is with us in our sufferings, but the God of open theism watches from a distance, wishing it were not happening, hoping (but not knowing) that something good can be rebuilt from the ashes. The God of the Bible has a track record that is perfect—he never, never fails. But the God of open theism fails us perhaps more often than we could possibly know—never meaning to, but failing nonetheless. The God of the Bible is big, but the God of open theism is just too small. Is it not clear, then, that the God of the Bible is simply not the God of open theism?

4

Open Theism and Prayer

The Openness View of Prayer

One of the major benefits of the open view, according to its supporters, is that prayer can be understood so much more personally and credibly.[1] What do they mean? Simply this: if God knows everything in the future, he always knows in advance anything and everything that we would bring to him in prayer. If so, this seems to make a mockery of the real personal relationship involved in prayer, because for anything we would pray, God would always think to himself, *Yes, I knew you would say that . . . Yes, I knew you would ask for that,* and so on. In other words, prayer could not function in our relationship with God in a way that actually affects what God thinks or possibly changes what he might do. If prayer cannot change things, what's the point? And if in prayer we say to God only what he has known from eternity that we would say or ask, then how dynamic and real can prayer be?

The solution, it seems to open theists, is to deny of God actual knowledge of what our prayers will be until we bring them to him. Yes, God knows all things past and present, but he cannot know the

future free actions and choices of his moral creatures until they perform those actions. And these future unknowns, of course, include
our prayers. For the sake of dynamic and real relationship with God,
and to underscore the authenticity of prayer that really matters, say
the open theists, we must move away from any model in which God
knows in advance all that we will ask or think. Greg Boyd describes
his vision of prayer like this:

> Because God wants us to be empowered, because he desires us to
> communicate with him, and because he wants us to learn depen-
> dency on him, he graciously grants us the ability to significantly
> affect him. This is the power of petitionary prayer. God displays his
> beautiful sovereignty by deciding *not* to always unilaterally decide
> matters. He enlists our input, not because he needs it, but because
> he desires to have an authentic, dynamic relationship with us as
> real, empowered persons. Like a loving parent or spouse, he wants
> not only to influence us but to be influenced *by us*.[2]

Real prayer means, then, that God learns our hearts' pleas as we pray
them to him, and that God can be affected by what we pray, so that
prayer really makes a difference.

UNDERSTANDING PRAYER BIBLICALLY

Does the open view of prayer accord with biblical teaching? As we
shall see, it simply does not. This is not to say that open theists are
wrong to affirm that prayer makes a difference. Surely it does! But I
hope it will be clear to readers that the way prayer makes a difference
is not as the open theist advocates. While this overview cannot be
exhaustive, let us consider a few principles of prayer that relate to the
openness proposal.

1. Perhaps we could start with the Lord's prayer as recorded in Matthew 6:9-13. Here, Jesus instructs his disciples, "Pray then like this:

"Our Father in heaven,
hallowed be your name.
Your kingdom come,
your will be done,
on earth as it is in heaven.
Give us this day our daily bread,
and forgive us our debts,
as we also have forgiven our debtors.
And lead us not into temptation,
but deliver us from evil."

Notice three things about this model prayer. First, it begins with an appeal to our Father in heaven, indicating the authority that God has over his children. Surely, the fatherly care of God is also communicated, but the initial stress is on his exalted position, his sacred name, and the rightful position of authority that he has over our lives. Second, this prayer does not assume that God's mind is yet to be made up. Jesus does not instruct us to pray, "your will be *formed*," but rather, "your will be *done*." God has a will that predates our prayers. There simply is no suggestion here that somehow our prayers help God shape his will, or that God is affected by our prayers in the very formation of his purposes. Rather, as we come to the Father in heaven, we recognize that our only appropriate place is to follow in the will of God, not to help shape it. So the prayer, "Your kingdom come, your will be done," is apt. Third, the daily dependence we should have on God in prayer is expressed with our daily request for bread. God's absolute authority over us, his fully-formed will that predates us, indicates that our place before him is one of utter dependence. Each and every day, we acknowledge to God that it is we who need him, and not he who in any sense needs us. God is the giver; we are the indebted recipients. We must never approach prayer or think of God in terms of what we contribute to God (cf. Acts 17:25, where God is not "served by human hands, as though he needed anything").

But doesn't this run counter to the impulse toward prayer encouraged by open theism? In the openness view, God waits to receive from us—our ideas, our longings, our desires—before he forms his will and chooses what is best to do. To see this, contrast Jesus' instruction in the Lord's prayer with this explanation of God's relationship with us from John Sanders:

> It is God's desire that we enter into a give-and-take relationship of love, and this is not accomplished by God's forcing his blueprint on us. Rather, God wants us to go through life together with him, making decisions together. Together we decide the actual course of my life. God's will for my life does not reside in a list of specific activities but in a personal relationship. As lover and friend, God works with us wherever we go and whatever we do. To a large extent our future is open and we are to determine what it will be in dialogue with God.[3]

I mean no disrespect when I ask, Whom should I believe: Jesus, or John Sanders? The contrast is that glaring. For Jesus, prayer with the Father was never a matter of deciding the actual course of his life together in dialogue with the Father. As he instructed his disciples to pray, "your will be done," so he lived his life. Recall that Jesus said, over and again, things like, "I do nothing on my own authority, but speak just as the Father taught me" (John 8:28), and, "I always do the things that are pleasing to him" (John 8:29). From beginning to end, Jesus sought to accomplish what his Father had sent him to do. Even in the garden, facing the biggest test of faith imaginable, Jesus prayed, "not my will, but yours, be done" (Luke 22:42).

The open view which portrays a kind of human autonomy and self-importance attaching to what *we* decide and what *we* bring to the Lord in prayer is altogether unfitting to the posture that Scripture enjoins us to have. We are to come before the exalted Father, not with our great ideas but with our humble and childlike requests, recognizing that these petitions are only as good as is their meshing with the already established will of God. Prayer is not given us by God to encourage our contribution to God's decision-making, but rather to enable our following of God's perfect and already formed will. "Your will be done" should echo through all godly, humble Christian praying.

2. The open theist notion that if God knows in advance what our prayers will be then prayer loses its authenticity, is itself called into question by Jesus' further instruction in Matthew 6. Look carefully at verses 31-33:

> Therefore do not be anxious, saying, 'What shall we eat?' or 'What shall we drink?' or 'What shall we wear?' For the Gentiles seek after all these things, and your heavenly Father knows that you need them all. But seek first the kingdom of God and his righteousness, and all these things will be added to you.

Well, how about that! Before you bring any of your requests to the Father, says Jesus, "your heavenly Father knows that you need them all"! For Jesus, acknowledgment of the Father's prior knowledge of our needs and hearts' desires does not diminish the meaningfulness or integrity of prayer; rather, God's prior knowledge of such things establishes the basis for Christian hope! It is precisely in knowing that God has had this problem in mind long before I have, that I can have hope when I pray. The fact is, I can never tell God something he doesn't know and didn't anticipate. And this fact inspires confidence, joy, and hope.

I recall a very special answer to prayer that God granted me during a summer trip to Israel. Our group had traveled by bus one very hot July day from Jerusalem to the Negev region, southeast toward the Dead Sea. That morning, I had read in my devotions the story of the Israelites wandering in the wilderness, living forty years in rocky, dry country like the one we were traveling in, and remarkably, I had noticed in my reading, God kept their shoes from wearing out (Deut. 29:5). As it turned out, we ourselves did a lot of walking that day, and I was glad that I was wearing the new sturdy boots I brought with me for just this purpose. On the way home, just before dusk, we stopped along the road to purchase some sodas. When we were all back in the bus, heading again toward Jerusalem, I reached for my camera to take a picture of a stunning red sunset settling over the desert landscape. I felt all around under my seat where I had put my camera, and it was gone. My seat was directly across from the bus door, and while everyone was getting their refreshments, evidently someone had reached in the bus and taken my camera.

My heart sank. This was my only camera, and one I had saved to purchase. It had in it a nearly completed roll of film, and I was deeply disappointed at the thought of losing the camera and those pictures. Well, at that moment I did what some people might think is ridiculous (in fact, I sort of thought so, too): I began praying that God would bring my camera back to me.

Of course, I realized how highly unlikely this would be. After all, there were probably thirty other people at the rest area where our bus had stopped, and we were now too far away to turn the bus around and go back. Whoever took my camera was probably miles away, and there simply would be no way to find out who took it or where they might have gone. I began to lose hope . . . and then I noticed the sole of the boot that crossed my leg. I stared at it in unbelief—here was a new and perfectly good boot, with strong Vibram soles, and yet this one day of hiking in the rocky Negev terrain had taken a toll on those boots. There were scars across the soles, and in places small chunks of the rubberized material was missing. The rugged rocks had done quite a number on these boots in one day's hike. And then the passage I had read that morning flooded my mind. I opened my Bible and read these words again in utter amazement: "I have led you forty years in the wilderness, Your clothes have not worn out on you, and *your sandals have not worn off your feet*" (Deut. 29:5, emphasis added). Forty years! And the same sandals lasted all that hiking and traveling! I stared at my boots and thought about this text. Wow, I thought, What a God!

This renewed my faith. I prayed again fervently that the God who could keep the children of Israel's sandals from wearing out for forty years would be the God who would bring my camera back to me.

A few miles up the road, our Arab driver pulled into an Israeli military compound, thinking that he could at least allow me to report the camera as missing. No one thought it would do any good, but it couldn't hurt. As we approached the main compound building, driving very slowly past a number of soldiers and trucks, off in the distance we heard a voice calling out something that none of us could understand. A few seconds later, we saw the person, far away, who was calling and was also running toward the bus. He had his right hand extended in the air, but at first we couldn't tell why. As he got closer, we could hear his words (in Hebrew), "Here it is, here it is!" he called. And what should he have in his hand, extended into the air, but my camera! As he approached the bus, the driver opened the door, and he handed to me the answer to my prayer.

And now I realize that the Father had evidently known of this future incident and my future prayer the morning that he led me to notice in Deuteronomy 29 (what I might have easily passed over) that the children of Israel's shoes did not wear out during their forty-year wandering. Before you ask, says Jesus, the Father already knows what you need. What strength to know that God already knows, and he is several steps ahead of us. He has planned the answer to our prayers before we pray. What folly to imagine that *real* prayer requires that God learn what we want only when we ask it. No, the God of the Bible knows and anticipates all that we ask. Our prayers do not inform him, but his answers can reveal, to the contrary, that he had long before undertaken to bring to us what we just now are bringing to him in prayer.

3. But doesn't God change his mind because of our prayers? Surely, it seems that Moses' intercession for Israel, for example, resulted in God changing what he said he would do (Ex. 32:11-14). So isn't prayer a means to affect God and redirect his plans? Consider the words of this passage, which follows the incident of the golden calf:

> But Moses implored the LORD his God and said, "O LORD, why does your wrath burn hot against your people, whom you have brought out of the land of Egypt with great power and with a

mighty hand? Why should the Egyptians say, 'With evil intent did he bring them out, to kill them in the mountains and to consume them from the face of the earth'? Turn from your burning anger and relent from this disaster against your people. Remember Abraham, Isaac, and Israel, your servants, to whom you swore by your own self, and said to them, 'I will multiply your offspring as the stars of heaven, and all this land that I have promised I will give to your offspring, and they shall inherit it forever.'" And the LORD relented from the disaster that he had spoken of bringing on his people.

While this is a favorite passage of open theists in their attempt to show that God can be persuaded by what we think, so much so that he even changes his mind about what he previously was going to do, we must ask, Could Moses actually have brought to God some insight, some perspective, some idea, that literally could have caused God to change his mind? How could this be? After all, as we look at what Moses prayed, we must acknowledge that absolutely everything he included in the "argument" of his prayer was already known by God. Consider Moses' three key points: 1) Why should you (God) destroy the very people you have saved with your mighty hand? 2) Why should you act toward Israel in a way that would make the Egyptians think you are evil? 3) Recall the covenant you made with Abraham, Isaac, and Jacob, in which you promised them and their seed blessing in the promised land forever. On which of these points would God have responded to Moses and said, "Say, Moses, good point. I just didn't understand it that way. Thanks for the insight—and for the reminder! I can hardly believe that I almost forgot about the covenant!"? But isn't it clear that, to understand this text in a way in which God literally changes his mind, something like this must be envisioned?

However, there are at least two crucial reasons for not going in this direction. First, the openness view proposes a humanizing of God that demeans his deity while it exalts our self-importance. And clearly, this is not the God of the Bible. Consider the sobering words of Isaiah 40:13-18, and may we all fall before God deeply and profoundly humbled:

Who has measured the Spirit of the LORD,
  or what man shows him his counsel?
Whom did he consult,
  and who made him understand?
Who taught him the path of justice,
  and taught him knowledge,
  and showed him the way of understanding?
Behold, the nations are like a drop from a bucket,
  and are accounted as the dust on the scales;
  behold, he takes up the coastlands like fine dust.
Lebanon would not suffice for fuel,
  nor are its beasts enough for a burnt offering.
All the nations are as nothing before him,
  they are accounted by him as less than nothing and emptiness.

To whom then will you liken God,
  or what likeness compare with him?

The God who declares, "my glory I give to no other" (Isa. 42:8), is the God who goes on record in Isaiah 40 that no one—absolutely *no one*—offers counsel to God. The point of saying that "the nations are like a drop from a bucket, and are accounted as the dust on the scales," is not that God doesn't care about the nations; rather, these words offer a comparison: in comparison to God's infinite knowledge and wisdom, in comparison to the vast and endless store of his understanding and the brilliance of his plans, the collective knowledge of the nations of the world amounts to a mere drop from a bucket; their collective wisdom is as inconsequential as specks of dust on the scales. Neither Moses nor you nor I can come to God in prayer and offer him some thought, some idea, some insight, some perspective, that could "counsel" him or provide a basis for God changing his mind.

Second, the openness view of our prayers effecting a literal change in God's mind misses the beauty and wonder of what actually is happening in a passage like Exodus 32.[4] This text, at this point, is not about a literal change in God's mind; it is about the kindness of God to involve his servant Moses in the fulfilling of his will. For here, as in so many of these "change of mind" passages, God deliberately tells his human servant of his threatened action, and God's telling this invites the servant to plead for mercy. God could have just brought judgment against wicked, sinful Israel without first telling Moses about it. But he *told* Moses about it in order to elicit from Moses the plea for mercy, by which God then carried out the mercy he originally intended, now in response to Moses' prayer. God's "change of mind," then, is actually the carrying out of the wider intention God had originally planned, but he did it by first proposing one thing in order to elicit Moses' involvement as he then did something different. Prayer, then, is a mechanism that invites our participation in the unfolding of the perfect and wise plan of God.

4. Does prayer make a difference? Yes, indeed, it does. But the reason prayer makes a difference is *not* that our prayers literally and

really change God's mind or plans. Recall that we are instructed to pray, "your will be done" (Matt. 6:10), and we are asked rhetorically, "Whom did he consult, and who made him understand?" (Isa. 40:14). In other words, we should pray acknowledging the previous and perfect plan of God that is already set (Matt. 6:10), and we should humbly admit that we can bring to God no insight or idea that could, in any way, contribute to the perfection of his understanding, knowledge, or wisdom (Isa. 40:14).

So, just how does our prayer make a difference? Simply put, in his kindness, God has designed that his good and perfect will be accomplished, in some respects, only as his people pray and first ask for God so to work. The role of prayer, then, becomes necessary to the accomplishing of these certain purposes, and our involvement in prayer, then, actually functions to assist in bringing these purposes to their fulfillment. God has designed some of his purposes to be accomplished *only* as we pray.

Now, why would God set things up this way? Why not just accomplish what he wishes, without the necessity of prayer? Here's the answer (are you ready to marvel?): God wants our participation with him in the work that he is doing, and so he "invented" prayer as a mechanism that draws us into the very anticipation and execution of the fulfillment of some of his purposes. Prayer invites our participation, and prayer involves our necessary (by God's design) role. Could God just "do it"? Yes, of course! But here is a God who shares bountifully with those whom he loves. And his sharing here is a sharing in the fulfillment of the plans and purposes he has set by his infinite wisdom and under his matchless authority (so we're not going to change God's mind—literally!). What kindness. What generosity. Prayer is one of God's tools to pull us into the center of the work that he has devised and is carrying out. By prayer, we long for what God's Spirit prompts us to pray, and as we pray according to his will, we anticipate and believe in the unfolding of just what God has designed to come about. When it does come about, our prayers are answered, we rejoice, God is glorified, and we understand better—from the inside, as it were—just what God had planned all along.

What a diminished view of God the openness proponents want us to accept. Their God is actually affected by the things that *we* want. Their God would literally change his plans and purposes because of what *we* think! Rather than finding these notions attractive, we should be horrified at such thoughts.[5] In contrast, the true God simply cannot (and should not!) literally be changed in what he perfectly, eternally, and infallibly has planned. But marvel: though he has planned all that he intends to do, he also has planned that our role in prayer provide for our entrance into the unfolding and accomplishment of some of his most precious infallible purposes. The God of the Bible is big—big enough to plan perfectly what he wills to be done while envisioning a way to involve little people like you and me in the unfolding of these purposes through prayers of longing, petition, anticipation, and hope. The God of open theism, by contrast, is small. And so, once again, we must conclude that the openness God is not the true and living God.

DIFFICULTIES WITH THE OPENNESS VIEW OF PRAYER

Having considered just some of Scripture's teaching on prayer as this relates to the openness proposal, it is now time to lay out some of the internal difficulties that this view of prayer faces. To be sure, every

Christian understanding of God and his relations to the world faces difficulties when it comes to explaining the nature and function of prayer.[6] But open theism faces a set of problems unique to it. That is, no other model of God and prayer throughout the history of the church has faced just what open theism faces here. This is so simply because no Christian tradition throughout history has ever denied that God knows the future exhaustively and definitely. But this denial is at the heart of what distinguishes open theism from all previous (and other) Christian understandings of God and the world, and this denial greatly affects its approach to prayer. So what are some of the special difficulties open theism faces on the question of the Christian's life of prayer?

1. Just how positive an idea is it that God wants to be influenced *by us,* as open theists claim? Clearly, this sounds good to our natural ears, since we live in a culture that tends to cater to what we want, a culture that tells us, "Have it your way." So naturally, we think it wonderful that not only Burger King but God himself wants, and waits, to know what we want. The customer rules, evidently, not only in the consumerism that drives our economy but also in the theology that proposes to reshape our churches.

Think about this a bit more. Consider what the notion of God wanting to be influenced by us requires. This must mean that God is willing to postpone planning many, many things until he finds out through prayer what his people want. If we are to take this seriously, then, we must imagine God as operating a sort of heavenly polling headquarters, receiving the "opinion polls" of our prayers as he seeks to decide what is best to do. My, what importance we have in the future of the world! What power prayer gives us! Since God waits to learn from us what we want, in countless numbers of cases (otherwise our prayers could not be said rightly to "significantly affect him"), our opinions turn out to be strategic in shaping the futures about which we pray, and we realize, then, just how significant we are to this world.

May I suggest that this notion plays well today because of the psychologized culture with which the Christian church is saturated. When self-esteem is the norm in our educational system, our children, including our Christian children, grow up with inordinate estimates of their self-importance. We urge them to "decide for themselves" at such early stages of life (so much for children honoring their fathers and mothers), and we are told not to correct them or tell them they are wrong but always and only applaud their efforts. So, is it any surprise that when open theists come along and say, "God respects you and your free will too much to decide the course of your life without your input; he waits to hear what you want before he makes his decisions," our natural ears hear this and say, "Well, of course!"

And here we see again what we see all through open theism: a high estimate of ourselves and a low estimate of God travel as a pair. And how tragic this is, in part because of the degrading of God that takes place, but also because of the false and harmful inflating of the value of our own ideas, opinions, desires, and longings that open theism ascribes to us. But please understand: I hope and pray that God never, never makes up his mind about something—whether about my life or anything else—based even in part on what I think or want! What chutzpah to think otherwise! Honestly, given my limited knowledge, finite and sinful perspective, diminutive wisdom, mixed moral compass, and fixation on the immediate—given all this and more, what a fool I would be if I thought that I had some idea, some thought, some insight that God should know before he makes up his mind! After all, who do I think I am, and who do I think God is! Open theism has gained a hearing, it seems clear to me, only because of the immensely low view of God and the unrealistically high view of self held in our churches and reinforced everywhere in our culture. All traditional views of God know better. And we can only pray that God will be gracious and help us to know better, too.

2. If this were not bad enough, here's another problem. The fact is, the God of open theism really cannot learn anything from our prayers, despite the advertising given to prayer in this model. After all, recall that open theism's deity knows *everything* past and present. Well, that means he knows all of the thought processes that have gone on in my mind over the past week, month, year, decade, and so on. He knows all that leads up to my formulating my prayer. So when I bring my prayer to him, there is no sense in which he can really interact with me in this prayer, as if he were learning just now what I am thinking and wanting. Rather, he is roughly in the same position as the God of traditional theism that openness proponents chide, i.e., the God who knows absolutely everything about absolutely everything. One thing is clear of the openness God: when I pray, because my prayer reflects my own thoughts, musings, desires—all of which God already knows perfectly—my prayer cannot be the sort of genuine interaction that they characterize it to be. The fact is, the God of open theism knows too much about me for his relationship with me to be "genuine" and "real."

So, where does this leave us? Essentially, open theists face another real problem with the notion that God chooses to be influenced by us when we pray. If he acts toward us as though he has actually "learned" something from our prayer, he must be kidding! A kind of divine condescension must be occurring if God hears my prayer and responds, "Well, that's interesting. And perhaps in light of this, I think that I had better change my mind about what I was planning." He cannot really mean it! Why? Simply because God already knows everything I (not to mention everyone else) have been thinking, wanting, longing for prior to the moment when I bring to him my prayer. Since God knows everything past and present, there is no possible way for me to bring him "new" information that could really affect his thinking about something. So the supposed "reality" and "genuineness" of God's relationship with us through prayer ends up being a sham—on openness standards, that is.

But whoever thought that the relationship between God and us would be the same as between two human persons? Isn't it possible for our relationship with God to be fully genuine and real, yet very different from our relationships with one another? It seems to me that, here again, open theism is employing a model of God that brings him down to our level. Unless God relates to us in the way we relate to each other, then there is no *real* relationship, we are told. How sad, and how demeaning to God. I wonder if the next generation of open theists, in recognizing this problem, may deny that God has exhaustive past and present knowledge also. How much more "real" our relationship with God would be if God didn't know my thoughts leading up to my prayer to him. Then, when I pray to God, I could actually tell him something that he doesn't know! How much better that would be! How much more *real* and *genuine* our relationship would be if each of us learned from each other what we each thought and wanted. Then God could be much more of a friend. And so we see the logic of the open view and the direction in which it presses.

3. Finally, given the fact that the God of open theism does have

exhaustive knowledge of the past and present (at least I know of no voices arguing for the direction speculated above), but that he lacks any knowledge of the future free choices and actions of his moral creatures, this God lacks knowledge that he needs to know in order to best answer our prayers. Consider long and hard these sobering words from David Basinger, an advocate of the open view:

> [W]e must acknowledge that divine guidance, from our perspective, cannot be considered a means of discovering exactly what will be best in the long run—as a means of discovering the very best long-term option. Divine guidance, rather, must be viewed primarily as a means of determining what is best for us now.[7]

And also:

> [S]ince God does not necessarily know exactly what will happen in the future, it is always possible that even that which God in his unparalleled wisdom believes to be the best course of action at any given time may not produce the anticipated results in the long run.[8]

Need more be said? These ideas, when expressed of God and not of your local financial advisor or even guidance counselor, take a true Christian's breath away! The staggering implications of this for one's confidence in God are almost more than one can bear. For consider, if God is good at short-range but not so hot with long-range forecasting, in which of these two categories (short-range or long-range) do most of our most significant fork-in-the-road decisions fall? How significant is it that we are here told that we best not look to God for the long-range matters—after all, the "anticipated results" may not be forthcoming, though they will always be well-intended? By bringing God down to the level of human frailty, we rob Christians of the confidence of knowing that God knows the end from the beginning, and that his answers to prayer and his guidance are always flawless. In the name of "genuine relationship" God has been dishonored and mocked. I can only imagine what the true and living God, the God of the Bible, thinks about this supposed portrayal of him.

Before leaving this last point, notice the dual nature of the problems the open view faces regarding prayer. Something of the horns of a dilemma are before openness proponents. On the one hand, because God knows the past and present exhaustively and accurately, he is simply *too knowledgeable and wise* to learn anything from our prayers. But on the other hand, because he lacks exhaustive definite knowledge of the future, he is *not knowledgeable and wise enough* to answer our most urgent and pressing prayers in the ways that are, in fact, best. Either direction one looks, the open view faces serious problems. Surely this indicates that we should look elsewhere for an understanding of the nature and purpose of prayer.

CLOSING STORY

We received a newsletter recently, sent out from CBInternational, a missions agency, recording the answered prayer of an unnamed missionary serving with CBI in Indonesia. The story goes like this:

> One Sunday I preached in seminary chapel in Indonesia on Romans 1:16, all the while praying, "Lord, give me chances to witness directly to the people here in the 'delicate' situation, proving that I too 'am not ashamed of the gospel.'" That night on the way

home from the city our Toyota, which had never failed us in eight years, stopped dead and refused to start.

Flashlight in hand, I was under the hood pretending to know something about cars when a voice hailed me from the sidewalk. "Can I help you? I am a Toyota repair man on my way home from work." Under his arm he carried a small bag. He took some wrenches from it and went to work before I had really answered him.

First he checked the gas to the carburetor because I was sure that was it. Next he checked the points, and when he did we saw in the darkness a spark flashing out of the coil. "Ah, that's it," he said, and proceeded to remove it.

Then, of all things, he took a brand new Toyota coil from his bag exactly the same size as the one he had just removed from my '89 Toyota. The only problem was that I had just spent the last of my cash to buy medicine for a needy student. So, we offered to take the mechanic home with us to get the needed money.

He was hardly in the car when he asked me, "Why are Christians always so easy to get to know?" I told him that even the Koran says that Christians were their "cousins'" closest friends. From there on he let me explain the whole gospel to him, right down to exactly what happened on the cross.

At my house, over tea and a cinnamon roll, we talked more. He seemed enthralled and offered no argument. Before his taxi came, I gave him a little booklet on how to find peace with God, my name, and my phone number and asked him to call me when he was ready to talk more.

This was surely a divine appointment. Our car stalling for the first time in eight years and a man walking by just after the car died, carrying a brand new Toyota coil in his bag was no accident.[9]

What joy to know that before we pray, the Father already knows what we need, and the Father has already set in motion the elements necessary for the answer to our prayers. This is not a God who learns what happens as things unfold; this is a God who unfolds what happens as he previously has known—and planned—that they will be. Prayer, to be genuine and real, to be dynamic and authentic, requires that God be working out his eternally fixed and perfect purposes in a manner in which he graciously involves us in his work through the vehicle of prayer. May God grant us eyes to see the glory of prayer, because through it, we see better the glory of the God "who works all things according to the counsel of his will" (Eph. 1:11).

5

OPEN THEISM AND HOPE

A MESSAGE OF "HOPE" FROM THE OPENNESS GOD

Imagine for a moment the excitement a young seminary graduate feels when he has finished years of rigorous study and preparation for ministry, and then he is called to serve as pastor of his first church. What a thrill! And what a joy! Now, imagine further that this graduate (we'll call him David) and his family move halfway across the country to pastor this church where, at first, things go well. There seems to be an endless supply of love and support for the new pastor and his family. But then, as these things sometimes go, a couple of people in the church begin complaining. Phone lines get filled with messages of resentment, and the warmth is now replaced with coldness and hardness. Imagine further with me that this young pastor is a humble, God-fearing man. David loves the Lord deeply, he endeavors to be faithful to Scripture in his preaching, and he tries to meet his pastoral responsibilities, given the constraints on his time. Nevertheless, the stirrings of discontent continue, and David now comes before God and cries out, "Lord, can you give me any basis for hope in this discouraging situation? And as I contemplate a lifetime of ministry, is there any reason to hope for better over the long term? Why did you lead me to such a discouraging place of ministry, and will it always be like this? Can I have hope that your purposes will prevail through these difficulties both now, and for my lifetime, and forever? God, please answer me. I desperately need some hope."

Now imagine what sort of response the *openness* God might offer this young pastor. Such a God might wish to tell David something like this: "David, the first thing I want you to know is that I love you. And I am deeply sorry about the misery these people in your church are causing you. I know your heart is right, and I know that their hearts are *not* right. I know this is very difficult, and I wish it weren't happening to you. But David, please don't blame me for what's happening. I know you sincerely sought my will in what church to pastor. And yes, I did give you strong indications that this church was the one of my choosing. To the best of my knowledge (as you know, I just cannot know a lot about what will happen in the future; in fact, I cannot know any of the myriad of free choices people will make in the future—but I am pretty good at anticipating what's most likely to happen) . . . to the best of my knowledge I thought this would be a good fit—you for them, and them for you. I guess that on this one I was wrong. I just didn't anticipate such bitterness and resentment from these people. After all, they're mostly young couples and young families, like you, and I hadn't seen any pattern of this kind of behavior before. Honestly, I am grieved over their behavior, and knowing what I know now, I regret leading you to take this pastorate. This is not the first time that I've had such regrets, though, and it most probably won't be the last. I have many regrets in my history of dealing with humans, and both you and I will just have to get used to this fact.

"Well, I know I haven't answered your questions directly, David, so now I'll try to. You asked first whether I could give you any basis for hope in this situation. Fair question, and I'll try to help you see things as I do. Yes, there is a basis for hope. You see, I do have ways to try to influence the situation. I can give thoughts to people that they might not have come up with on their own, and I can try to help them see the consequences of their words and actions. But the problem, of course, is that I just don't know whether my attempts to influence them will achieve the desired effect. Sometimes I succeed at this, but sometimes I fail. I just don't know whether things will get better—or worse! But, I can promise you that I'll do my best. Now you might wonder if I could simply overrule their free wills and just make them behave! Well, I really can't do that and still respect their personal integrity. If I started doing this, there would be no end of it! So many things go wrong moment by moment (just think for a minute of how many people—all free to do as they please—there are in the world, and how many horrible things are done to others every moment around the whole world; and I see every one of them and grieve over them), and so many times I feel deep disappointment and distress. So, you can see that if I went down this path of 'correcting' all the problems I see, well, I might as well just abandon the whole idea of having a creation with free moral beings. So, I do my best, but obviously I simply cannot guarantee that things will change. However, I *can* promise you that I'll be with you every day in the future just as I've been with you in the past! All that I am is there for you, and this should give you hope.

"And David, by the way, please don't try to figure out some 'divine purpose' behind your situation. Things like this just happen. I do my best to bring some good out of these messes, but again, I just can't guarantee whether good will come of it or not. I'll try to help with everything that I can, but so much of this depends on how both you and a host of other free persons choose to act. I just don't know (now) how you and others will act, so I can't say (now) whether any good—or further bad!— will come from it. So my advice is, don't get your hopes up for any good to come from your current situation. If it does, we'll both be grateful, but there simply are no guarantees. You're really best off just to accept all the difficulties and trials in your life as pointless.

"Now, you asked another question that, frankly, I wish you hadn't brought up. You asked about hope as you anticipate a whole lifetime of ministry. This simply is not a fair question. You see, I'm pretty good with short-range matters, but with long-range issues, I just am unable to give sound advice. People ask me questions like this all the time, and I simply wish they'd realize that these are not fair questions. If you want assurances that somehow, your ministry forty years from now will be fruitful, how could I know that? To be honest, I don't even know now whether you'll be alive forty years from now, or alive tomorrow, for that matter (maybe a drunk driver will plow into you head-on as you drive home from your office today—I just don't know). You see, you simply must come to grips with the fact that *I cannot know what free creatures will choose and do before they make their own free choices and perform their own free actions.* Now, if you think about this a bit, and realize how many choices and actions take place every single second, and then how many other choices and other actions flow from the earlier ones, and then still more choices and actions flow from those, and so on and so on, and because each time the choices and actions are free, they all could have been different choices and actions from what they turn out to be—well, you begin to see just how impossible it is for me to give anything close to accurate predictions of things far off. Now, don't get me wrong. I can, with my infinite intelligence, think of all the possibilities! What a staggering assortment of possibilities there are! But, of this vast assortment, I absolutely cannot know which set of choices and actions will comprise the one that will happen in the future. And the further out you go, the crazier it gets!

"Frankly, this is exactly why I make the mistakes I do. When I make a decision about something relating to human beings, they can always do things I didn't expect, and so I can end up being quite shocked at what they do and regretting my own actions. Boy, did that very first sin in the garden of Eden take me aback! Can you imagine, after giving Adam and Eve all that I did, and being so kind and generous—well, who would have thought that . . . ? Enough already. I still can't believe they turned from me. And that was just the beginning of the surprises! What a ride this has been!

"So, David, settle with the realization that we're in this together day by day. We both have to make lots of adjustments—changing constantly from plan Q to plan R to plan S, and so on. There just are no guarantees for the future, except for you to know that I'll be there with you. So we'll work together at making the best decisions we can along the way, and the working together is what matters the most anyway.

"I'm glad that you also asked about 'forever.' Here's one place where I can assure you that my purposes will be accomplished. I *will* win in the end! You know, one of the main reasons that I designed 'the creation project' as I have is so that, in the end, there might be a host of people who love and worship me forever. And the time will come when I'll just bring the current course of history to an end. At that point, things will be set and nothing can change it. So, please know that my ultimate purposes are certain.

"Now, I guess I'd better say just a bit more, because I don't want to give you the wrong impression. When I bring the current course of history to an end, what I cannot do at that point is change what has happened earlier. After all, I gave people their free wills, and I wasn't able to know (and I still can't know) what free people would do with that freedom. So, at whatever point I 'end' history as we know it, I'll have to accept at that point what all those who have lived and made free choices have done with their freedom. So when I say that 'things will be set,' you shouldn't understand this to mean that everything will finally come together, if you will, exactly as I had in mind. I'm hopeful, of course. But what I mean is simply that, at some point, I'll just end the flow of history that we're in now, and people will be assigned their respective destinies, and however many have accepted my love will be accepted into heaven, and the others will be lost eternally.

"Of course, this raises the question of how well things are going so far—in terms of my wooing people so that they know my love and love me in return. Well, frankly, I haven't thought it best to bring an end to history yet. If you look around the world, evil is rampant and there is such a scarcity of true love. If I were to command history to stop now, I'm not sure I would want to accept what I'd get—not yet, anyway. So, I'm letting it go longer, and I'm hopeful that many more people will see my love for them and will love me in return. Now, if you were to ask if I could be sure that a certain number of people will be 'saved' in the end, well, that's a question I just cannot answer. One can certainly look at the world as it is now and see how I have 'succeeded' to date! But I *am* hoping for a great improvement. And because I'm in control of when history will end and can dictate when my purposes for the present world will be concluded, there is great reason for you to put hope in me for the 'forever' you asked about. I am God, after all, and I reign sovereign over the kind of creation I made and over its conclusion. Of course, what sort of things happen in human affairs *between* my sovereign acts to create and to consummate history is largely up to free agents, whose actions I cannot know in advance.

"Well, David, I hope you see what hope there is when you put your faith in me. I hope you see that you are in good hands when you place your life, your wife, your children, your most cherished dreams and visions into my hands. And the good news is that the hope you have in me is the very same hope every child of mine may have in me! All of my children may have the confidence in knowing that the same care and love expressed toward you, David, is also expressed toward them. For now, for your lives on into the future (however long that may be), and forever—place your hope in me!"

OUR TRUE HOPE IN THE TRUE AND LIVING GOD

There is much to be said about real and genuine hope in God. The God of the Bible, the true and living God, deeply longs and calls for his people to put their hope in him alone, and to do so with a deep and abiding sense of confidence, peace, and joy. The hope in God that is undermined by the openness proposal is the very hope that God wants his people to have. The true God does not make mistakes. He doesn't second-guess the wisdom of his own past actions. He is not taken by surprise as human history unfolds. He doesn't wonder how things will work out. He designs good purposes in the trials of life. And all of his plans and purposes are right on course. He knows the end from the beginning, and so he knows how each and every circumstance of life contributes to the fulfillment of his matchless purposes.

The God of the Bible wants to provide true and lasting hope for his children for the present and for the long-range future and for all eternity. In each of these stages of our lives, God wants us to put our hope, confidently and exclusively, in him. In what follows, then, we will consider three biblical expressions of hope in God, each focusing on a different "stage" of life. Psalm 62 enjoins us to hope in God in the present, even when we face great difficulties. In Romans 4 Paul presents Abraham as one whose hope in God extended far into the future. Then, 1 Peter 1 will help us set our sights on the life to come. Life now, life over our future years, and life forever—all these are meant to be lived in deep and abiding hope in our glorious and gracious God.

Meditation on Hope for Today (Psalm 62)

(1) For God alone my soul waits in silence;
   from him comes my salvation.
(2) He only is my rock and my salvation, my fortress;
   I shall not be greatly shaken.
(3) How long will all of you attack a man to batter him,
   like a leaning wall, a tottering fence?
(4) They only plan to thrust him down from his high position.
   They take pleasure in falsehood.
They bless with their mouths,
   but inwardly they curse. Selah
(5) For God alone, O my soul, wait in silence,
   for my hope is from him.

(6) He only is my rock and my salvation,
my fortress; I shall not be shaken.
(7) On God rests my salvation and my glory;
my mighty rock, my refuge is God.
(8) Trust in him at all times, O people;
pour out your heart before him;
God is a refuge for us. *Selah*
(9) Those of low estate are but a breath;
those of high estate are a delusion;
in the balances they go up;
they are together lighter than a breath.
(10) Put no trust in extortion;
set no vain hopes on robbery;
if riches increase, set not your heart on them.
(11) Once God has spoken;
twice have I heard this:
that power belongs to God,
(12) and that to you, O LORD, belongs steadfast love.
For you will render to a man
according to his work.

Psalm 62, a psalm of David, expresses hope for God's salvation (vv. 1-2, 6-7) amid the affliction he currently endures. What undergirds his hope, most fundamentally, is the strength and power of God, in which he is protected as a man in a fortress (vv. 2, 6; cf. v. 8) or as one standing on an unshakable rock (vv. 2, 6), and the steadfast love of God for his own, as expressed at the end of the psalm (v. 12). The contrast between the supremacy of God and the feebleness of men, including the feebleness of those who oppose God, is made clear. Verse 9 points to both those of "low estate" and those of "high estate" as "together lighter than a breath." Neither those low nor those high, nor both together, can bring any challenge to David's refuge, the almighty God. Verses 11-12 underscore the greatness of God: "Once God has spoken; twice have I heard this: that power belongs to God, and that to you, O LORD, belongs steadfast love." The phrase "once . . . twice" expresses the superlative quality of God over all who would stand against him. His greatness, power, and love are supreme. The psalmist has great reason to hope, because the one in whom he hopes is the one and only God over all.

Notice also the exclusive nature of the psalmist's hope: "For God *alone* my soul waits. . . . He *only* is my rock and my salvation" (vv. 1-2; repeated with minor variation in vv. 5-6). And besides these explicit expressions of God's exclusive claim on his hope, the psalmist repeatedly emphasizes, "on *God* rests my salvation" (v. 7a), "my refuge is *God*" (v. 7b), "trust in *him* at all times, O people" (v. 8a), "*God* is a refuge for us" (v. 8b), "power belongs to *God*" (v. 11), and "to you, O LORD, belongs steadfast love" (v. 12).[1]

What is the basis of hope for today, according to David? Consider the following elements. First, God is greater and mightier than any and all of the human powers that stand against David. In fact the contrast between the power of God and that of mere humans is so great that David says the collective power of men is "lighter than a breath" (v. 9). This brings to mind other such expressions in Scripture. As we observed earlier, Isaiah 40:15, for example, compares the totality of the prowess and might of the nations of the world with "a drop from a bucket" or "dust on the scales." Similarly, the chastened Nebuchadnezzar, king of the mighty Babylon, after learning that "the Most High rules the kingdom of men and gives it to whom he will" (Dan. 4:32) compares this mighty God to the nations of the world and says that, in comparison to God, "all the inhabitants of the earth are accounted as nothing" (Dan. 4:35). Immeasurably great confidence and hope in God come from knowing the matchless extent of his power over all. To be in *this* fortress that is God makes all the difference.

Second, because God is immeasurably mighty, what comfort and peace can come from resting in him! No wonder the psalmist's soul can wait in silence (Ps. 62:1, 5) before him. Here, all worrying and scurrying cease. To know this is to know that we "shall not be greatly shaken" (vv. 2, 6). In other words, David is confident that no matter what attacks (v. 3) or cursings (v. 4) he experiences, he cannot be shaken from his place of rest in the mighty fortress who is his God.

Third, if God were not so capable and mighty, we might be tempted to go elsewhere for counsel or for help; we might seek to find even devious ways to secure what we want. But David says, first, "trust in [God] at all times, O people; pour out your heart before him; God is a refuge for us" (v. 8), and then, "put no trust in extortion; set no vain hopes on robbery; if riches increase, set not your heart on them" (v. 10). We serve a God of whom we can be so sure, that we would be fools to trust in other measures. There is no more confident place to be than under the watchful care of this God.

The contrast with open theism's proposed deity could not be more marked. Here we have a God whose power and love are unexcelled, and his protection and care for his own are sure. Of course this does not remove from God's people the possibility of attacks and opposition, but it does remove the possibility that these feeble human forces—who are "together lighter than a breath" (v. 9b)—can cause any harm or inflict any injury that God would not superintend in fulfillment of his purposes. The psalm ends with the reassurance of God's indomitable power and overwhelming love, alongside the certainty of his holding each person accountable for his or her

119

actions. We have hope in God, for his protection now, and for the certainty that his judgment will reign in the day to come. The openness God pales, by comparison. Compare the God of the Bible and the openness deity on questions of the divine power, wisdom, purpose, and genuine love. Without any doubt, the God of open theism is just too small.

Meditation on Hope for the Long Haul (Romans 4:18-21)

(18) In hope [Abraham] believed against hope, that he should become the father of many nations, as he had been told, "So shall your offspring be." (19) He did not weaken in faith when he considered his own body, which was as good as dead (since he was about a hundred years old), or when he considered the barrenness of Sarah's womb. (20) No distrust made him waver concerning the promise of God, but he grew strong in his faith as he gave glory to God, (21) fully convinced that God was able to do what he had promised.

Can true hope sustain us over the long haul? One of Scripture's finest examples of lifelong hope is Abraham. Paul extols the persistent faith of Abraham not only because he believed that God would do what was humanly impossible (to bring a child from this "dead" and "barren" elderly couple), but also because he persisted in his faith for such a long time. Imagine the struggle Abraham must have faced as he observed Sarah, and his own body, move past their respective abilities to become parents. But according to Paul, Abraham not only did not weaken in faith as the years went by and the promise was yet unfulfilled and their physical inability became more evident: he actually *grew strong in his faith.* Over the years, he became more fully convinced that God was able to do what he had promised. Here we have not just hope for today but hope for the long term. And we should be led to wonder, on what is this strong, vibrant, enduring hope in God based?

Essentially, the two qualities of God that sustained Abraham's hope over these many years were God's *wisdom* and his *power*. You can see these in Romans 4:21 where we read that Abraham was "fully convinced that God was *able* [God's power] to do what he had *promised* [God's wise plan]" (emphasis added). Deep and abiding hope in God requires confidence in these two qualities of God. First, God's wisdom must be unexcelled and perfect. If we worry that God's plans might falter, or that God might get things wrong, or that God might second-guess what he has planned, this will undermine all hope in God. For a vibrant hope, we must know that God's plans are best, and that even if we can't understand them and can't see how they will be fulfilled, we know God, and we know that his ways are, always and without exception, infinitely wise. But second, we also must have the confidence that God is able to accomplish what his wisdom has planned. It is one thing for God to promise what he alone knows is best, but if we have reason to doubt God's ability to accomplish what he has promised, we will not have a viable hope. Abraham's hope is remarkable for its persevering conviction regarding both the wisdom of God (his plan and promise are unsurpassed) and the power of God (he is able to do what he said he would, despite the human impossibility of it happening).

Notice one other element of Abraham's experience that shows the quality of true hope in God. Verse 19 tells us that Abraham "did not weaken in faith when *he considered* his own body, which was as good as dead (since he was about a hundred years old), or when *he considered* the barrenness of Sarah's womb" (emphasis added). True hope in God does not focus on the obstacles to God's accomplishment of his work, but it also does not ignore them. Remarkably, Abraham *considered* both his own aging body and its attending impotence (which is the likely meaning of "as good as dead") and the inability of Sarah to conceive a child. He took full stock of the problems faced in God's doing what he had promised. He was not an advocate of positive thinking who refused even to acknowledge the problems that were before him, but neither was he a pessimist, an "Eeyore" if you will, who got so lost in the magnitude of the problems that his hope vanished. No, Abraham seriously considered the reality of the problem—and what a problem it was! Neither he nor Sarah could become parents, and God's promise required that they do just this! But despite these problems, Abraham believed that God is wise (the plan and promise are of God's own devising and so are best) and that God is powerful (he is able to do even the impossible here, since he can, as verse 17 indicates, bring life from the dead).

Again, when one considers hope for the long haul and compares the God of the Bible and the God of open theism, we can see such notable contrasts. Imagine if Abraham had accepted the openness view of God! Since God's plans can be mistaken, and God can find in retrospect that things he thought would be best perhaps are not best, would not Abraham have reason to begin questioning both God's wisdom and his promise? And if God is not all-wise, then hope in him is undermined. What if Abraham had considered God's purposes seldom to "interfere" with the laws of nature that he established (another openness theme)? Wouldn't he rightly begin to wonder whether God lacked (by his own choice in creating the kind of world he did) the power to accomplish what he had promised? After all, perhaps God had intended for this promise to be fulfilled while both Abraham and

Sarah were biologically able to have children, and God just didn't know that they would become impotent and barren as quickly as they did. If the God Abraham trusted had been the God of open theism, I'm afraid that instead of moving from one level of hope to a yet stronger one (v. 18), he would have been tempted toward despair.

But to read Romans 4:18-21 is to see unshakable confidence and hope in both God's wisdom and his power. Since both of these qualities are irreparably damaged by the open view of God, we must conclude that Abraham's faith simply could not have been in the open-view deity. As Abraham surely would testify, *that* God would be simply too small for *this* promise and *this* fulfillment to occur. Hope for the long haul requires deep and abiding confidence that God always gets it right, that his ways are perfect, his wisdom is impeccable, and his power is always able to accomplish what his wisdom has planned. This is the foundation for a lifetime of hope, and this is the hope we see in Abraham.

Meditation on Hope for Eternity (1 Peter 1:3-9)

(3) Blessed be the God and Father of our Lord Jesus Christ! According to his great mercy, he has caused us to be born again to a living hope through the resurrection of Jesus Christ from the dead, (4) to an inheritance that is imperishable, undefiled, and unfading, kept in heaven for you, (5) who by God's power are being guarded through faith for a salvation ready to be revealed in the last time. (6) In this you rejoice, though now for a little while, as was necessary, you have been grieved by various trials, (7) so that the tested genuineness of your faith—more precious than gold that perishes though it is tested by fire—may be found to result in praise and glory and honor at the revelation of Jesus Christ. (8) Though you have not seen him, you love him. Though you do not now see

him, you believe in him and rejoice with joy that is inexpressible and filled with glory, (9) obtaining the outcome of your faith, the salvation of your souls.

Notice three aspects of our hope for the future. First, the hope we have from the God and Father of our Lord Jesus Christ is a "living hope" (1 Pet. 1:3). As Christ was raised from the dead and so lives, so we too, who are born again through his death and resurrection, likewise enter into eternal life. Hence, our hope is a living, lasting, enduring, eternal hope. Nothing can "kill" this hope, and it will go on as long as eternity lasts—forever! The hope we have now lives on, because it is founded on the everlasting life of the risen Lord.

Second, an indication of the future reality of our living and eternal hope is the inheritance awaiting us (v. 4). Peter describes it as an imperishable, undefiled, and unfading inheritance, kept in heaven for us. While Peter surely is connecting the future reception of the inheritance with our present faith, his stress is on what awaits us then. And not only is our inheritance being kept for us, we ourselves are being guarded by God's own power through faith for the future salvation that will one day be revealed. Our "living hope" will not disappoint simply because that in which our hope is set (i.e., God, who raised Christ from the dead) has secured both us and our inheritance for a day yet coming. The surety of God's power to guard us for our own future salvation, and to secure for us our eternal inheritance, is a strong basis for our eternal hope—a hope that will never be dismayed.

Third, the testings and trials of our faith in this life should be seen, in light of eternity, as "more precious than gold that perishes" (vv. 6-7). What an astonishing view of these trials! Far from decrying trials and affliction, Peter would have us rejoice in them, since they will be cause for "praise and glory and honor at the revelation of Jesus Christ" (v. 7). Does this not require a view that the trials of this life are purposeful? Does this not demand our trust in God to orchestrate the tribulation of our lives so that praise and honor are produced through them? So far from "pointless suffering"[2] is this view, that it exposes the facile and hurtful posture of open theism toward suffering. What harm is done to Christian faith and life when the very divinely ordained purpose of suffering is expunged from it. For Peter, suffering is a reality that Christians face in their allegiance to Christ, and how wonderful to know that the growth of our faith through this suffering has an eternal glory and an eternal reward.

CONCLUSION

Once again, we see how far short the open view falls when put next to biblical teaching on hope. Whether hope for today, for a lifetime, or for eternity, the hope of Scripture is based on the certainty of God's work and the unfailing accomplishment of his wise and good purposes and plans. Where open theism reduces our hope to something unavoidably fragile and weak, the Bible commends a hope that is strong, secure, fixed, and certain. Life is purposeful, and the God who gives himself to us is the conquering God who will lead us in his triumph. Our hope is secure, it is filled with joy and peace, and it will last eternally.

Recall, as we conclude, the "Message of 'Hope' from the Openness God" with which we began this chapter, and contrast this vision of God and its corresponding hope to what we see over and again in Scripture. Whereas the God of open theism discourages us from thinking of any good purpose being served in times of suffering, the God of the Bible wants us always to know that his good and wise hand directs and his wise (if hidden) purposes will be fulfilled. The openness God unavoidably makes all kinds of mistakes—mistakes in his guidance, mistakes in his dealings with free moral agents, mistakes in his own actions and responses—but the true God chooses perfectly, designs flawlessly, and accomplishes his will as he alone knows is best. The openness God cannot guarantee whether eternity will be what he hopes it will be, any more than he can guarantee that he'll get what he wants now, or in the immediate future, or in the distant future; the true God's plans are set, and he knows, from before he created, all that will occur and how he will fulfill all of his intentions. The openness God allows himself to be vulnerable before hostile moral forces from human and demonic sources, sometimes losing when he wished he had won, and always in doubt as to whether his purposes or Satan's might prevail in any given situation; the true God reigns over Satan, his demons, and over everything in the heavens and on the earth, assuring his followers of the victory that is theirs also as they rest in him. And at the root of it all, the openness God cannot know the future free choices and actions of his moral creatures, but the true God knows all exhaustively and definitely, past, present, and future. The certainty of hope that is founded in the true and living God is simply diminished and defeated by open theism's understanding of God. For the sake of vibrant Christian hope, for now and throughout life and for eternity, may God give us eyes to see and hearts to embrace the true and living God, to the glory of his name.

CONCLUSION

We began this study by observing that both the *glory of God* and the genuine *good of his children* are irreparably harmed in open theism's novel proposal. God, as we have seen, is made to look much more like us—wondering whether his plans will work, second-guessing the wisdom of his past actions, wishing that a multitude of things might have worked out differently, and struggling to give the best advice and assistance he can to his children given the manifold uncertainties that both he and they face. And in the process we, his children, are made to look somewhat more godlike: responsible for actually shaping the future histories of our lives by the choices we make (which God learns about only as we make them); influencing God, even endeavoring to compel him to change his mind as in prayer we tell him what we think; and in the end embracing a bit more "human sovereignty" (as it might be called) and feeling a bit more in charge of our own destinies and more capable of shaping the outcome of history. In all of this, the luster and brilliance of God's glory is smudged beyond recognition, and the real good of humans is replaced by the apparent exalted dignity and self-empowerment we assert for ourselves at God's expense.

Bear in mind, however, that this divine demotion and human exaltation is in appearance only. No theological proposal, no matter how far off center biblically it may be, can affect the truth about who God *really* is or the truth about who we humans *really* are. But great harm here befalls our view of God, our hope, and our confidence in God's word and promise. And through this diminishing of our view of God, our true strength, joy, peace, and holiness are ravaged. The diminishing of the glory of God is the *cause* of the harm done to our spiritual well-being. A. W. Tozer spoke powerfully and prophetically when he wrote,

> Let us beware lest we in our pride accept the erroneous notion that idolatry consists only in kneeling before visible objects of adoration, and that civilized peoples are therefore free from it. The essence of idolatry is the entertainment of thoughts about God that are unworthy of Him. It begins in the mind and may be present where no overt act of worship has taken place. . . .
>
> Perverted notions about God soon rot the religion in which they appear. The long career of Israel demonstrates this clearly enough, and the history of the Church confirms it. So necessary to the Church is a lofty concept of God that when that concept in any measure declines, the Church with her worship and her moral standards declines along with it. The first step down for any church is taken when it surrenders its high opinion of God.[1]

This was written several decades before open theism's current God-belittling proposal; one can only imagine what A. W. Tozer would say today to the new idolatry of open theism. Sadly, Tozer is no longer with us. And yet, with his vision and his passion, we too can commend the exalted and glorious view of the true God, and by this bless those who then behold his real beauty, splendor, and majesty. Again,

Tozer's admonition to Christians is undoubtedly more urgent today than when he penned these words:

> The heaviest obligation lying upon the Christian Church today is to purify and elevate her concept of God until it is once more worthy of Him—and of her. In all her prayers and labors this should have first place. We do the greatest service to the next generation of Christians by passing on to them undimmed and undiminished that noble concept of God which we received from our Hebrew and Christian fathers of generations past. This will prove of greater value to them than anything that art or science can devise.[2]

Here, then, are the questions before us: Will we bring harm or blessing to our generation and the next? What view of God will we and our children embrace? Will our view of God lead both us and the next generation to higher views of self and diminished views of God? Or will we truly worship, honor, trust, hope in, obey, and follow the true God of Scripture? Will we echo our culture's quest for self-esteem and by this miss the biblical vision and joy of an all-consuming God-esteem? Or will we bow humbly before the all-knowing, exalted God of heaven and earth and acknowledge that his will and ways alone are right? In short, will we be idolaters, or will we honor God as he is?

The open view of God proposes a challenge to the evangelical church that is unparalleled in this generation. May our earnest prayer and unceasing effort be to advance the knowledge of the God who *is.* So then, for the magnifying of his name, and for the joy, blessing, strength, and wholeness of God's people, "let us press on to know the LORD" (Hos. 6:3).

NOTES

CHAPTER 1
OPEN THEISM AND THE CHRISTIAN FAITH

1. Gregory A. Boyd, *God of the Possible: A Biblical Introduction to the Open View of God* (Grand Rapids, Mich.: Baker, 2000), 102.

2. In Bruce A. Ware, *God's Lesser Glory. The Diminished God of Open Theism* (Wheaton, Ill.: Crossway, 2000), I discuss two broad categories of passages appealed to by open theists: "divine growth in knowledge texts" (65-86); and "divine repentance texts" (86-98). The two examples that follow provide one passage from each category.

3. Boyd, *God of the Possible*, 62.

4. John Sanders, *The God Who Risks: A Theology of Providence* (Downers Grove, Ill.: InterVarsity, 1998), 50.

5. Ware, *God's Lesser Glory*, 65-141.

CHAPTER 2
OPEN THEISM AND GOD'S FOREKNOWLEDGE

1. John Sanders, *The God Who Risks: A Theology of Providence* (Downers Grove, Ill.: InterVarsity, 1998), 52-53.

2. Gregory A. Boyd, *God of the Possible: A Biblical Introduction to the Open View of God* (Grand Rapids, Mich.: Baker, 2000), 56.

3. Sanders, *God Who Risks*, 50.

4. For a much more extensive discussion of both of these lines of response, the reader may wish to consult my larger critique of open theism in which

I devote two full chapters to these questions. See Bruce A. Ware, *God's Lesser Glory: The Diminished God of Open Theism* (Wheaton, Ill.: Crossway, 2000), chapters 4 (65-98) and 5 (99-141).

5. See, for example, Boyd, *God of the Possible,* 54, 60, 67, 71-72, and 120.

6. Sanders, *God Who Risks,* 50.

7. Isaiah 41:21-29; 42:8-9; 43:8-13; 44:6-8; 44:24-28; 45:20-23; 46:8-11; 48:3-8; 48:14-16.

8. For openness discussions of biblical prophecy, see Sanders, *God Who Risks,* 129-137; Richard Rice, *God's Foreknowledge and Man's Free Will* (Minneapolis: Bethany, 1985), 75-81; Richard Rice, "Biblical Support for a New Perspective," in Clark Pinnock, Richard Rice, John Sanders, William Hasker, and David Basinger, *The Openness of God: A Biblical Challenge to the Traditional Understanding of God* (Downers Grove, Ill.: InterVarsity, 1994), 50-53; and David Basinger, "Can an Evangelical Christian Justifiably Deny God's Exhaustive Knowledge of the Future?" *Christian Scholar's Review* 25 (1995), 141.

9. E-mail message by Chelsea DeArmond, sent to members of a discussion list, from edgrenfellowship@yahoo.com, Friday, February 2, 2001, at 3:50 p.m.

10. For further discussion of the Jonah prediction, see Ware, *God's Lesser Glory,* 90-98.

11. Boyd (*God of the Possible,* 40) comments that, "even if this verse [Ps. 139:16] said that the exact length of our lives was settled before we were born, it wouldn't follow that *everything* about our future was settled before we were born." However, even if we were to grant that God does not foreknow absolutely everything, even the amount of what *must* be foreknown—most of which includes future free choices and actions—to know *that* we will live a certain number of days, is staggering.

12. In several public discussions of open theism, with prominent open theists in the room, I have asked for an openness accounting of Daniel, and of Daniel 11 in particular. All I have received to date are blank stares. And it is no wonder why this is. With such detailed and exacting predictions that involve innumerable free future human choices and actions, over so many centuries, and involving so many people and nations, there simply is no way to account for these predictions without 1) resorting to the liberal "late dating" of Daniel; 2) holding that God meticulously controlled what happened so that those who performed those actions were not really free and responsible, as openness pro-

ponents understand this; or 3) believing that God really did know and predict what free human persons would do. Clearly, the last answer is called for by the passage, but none of the three possibilities is at all appealing to open theists.

13. Boyd, *God of the Possible,* 35-37.

14. I wish to thank Ted Griffin at Crossway Books for pointing out this text and its significance to Bill Deckard and me in relation to the openness proposal, and I am grateful also for helpful comments by Ardel Caneday and Tom Schreiner on this brief meditation.

15. Ardel B. Caneday, "Veiled Glory: God's Self-Revelation in Human Likeness—A Biblical Theology of God's Anthropomorphic Self-Disclosure," in John Piper, Justin Taylor, and Paul K. Helseth, eds., *Beyond the Bounds: Open Theism and the Undermining of Biblical Christianity* (Wheaton, Ill.: Crossway, 2003), 185-186.

CHAPTER 3
OPEN THEISM AND SUFFERING

1. Westminster Confession of Faith, III.1.

2. Eric Zorn, news report online at: http://www.nd.edu/~ndmag/zornau95.html.

3. Toby Willis, "Why?" online at: http://www.hopeway.org/gospel/why.asp. Good News Publishers has also produced a version of the Willises' story as an evangelistic tract titled "Through the Flames," which can be read and ordered at: http://www.gnpcb.org/product/663575724360.

4. Mark Gillmore, "How Could They Make It?" online at: http://www.gnn.net/silent/howcould.html.

5. Gregory A. Boyd, *God of the Possible: A Biblical Introduction to the Open View of God* (Grand Rapids, Mich.: Baker, 2000), 103-106.

6. Ibid., 105.

7. Ibid., 105-106.

8. Sanders, *The God Who Risks: A Theology of Providence* (Downers Grove, Ill.: InterVarsity, 1998), 261-262.

9. C. S. Lewis, *The Problem of Pain* (New York: Macmillan, 1959), 81.

10. Sanders, *God Who Risks,* 262.

11. Boyd, *God of the Possible,* 106.

CHAPTER 4
OPEN THEISM AND PRAYER

1. For defenses of open theism's view of prayer, see David Basinger, "Practical Implications," chapter 5 of Clark Pinnock, Richard Rice, John Sanders, William Hasker, and David Basinger, *The Openness of God: A Biblical Challenge to the Traditional Understanding of God* (Downers Grove, Ill.: InterVarsity, 1994), 156-162; John Sanders, *The God Who Risks: A Theology of Providence* (Downers Grove, Ill.: InterVarsity, 1998), 268-274; and Gregory A. Boyd, *God of the Possible: A Biblical Introduction to the Open View of God* (Grand Rapids, Mich.: Baker, 2000), 95-98.

2. Boyd, *God of the Possible,* 96 (emphasis in original).

3. Sanders, *God Who Risks,* 277.

4. For elaboration on this perspective, see Bruce A. Ware, *God's Lesser Glory: The Diminished God of Open Theism* (Wheaton, Ill.: Crossway, 2000), 90-98.

5. See more on this notion in the discussion below.

6. To see how prayer is understood within various models of divine providence, and the specific problems it faces within each model respectively, see Terrance Tiessen, *Providence and Prayer: How Does God Work in the World?* (Downers Grove, Ill.: InterVarsity, 2000).

7. Basinger, "Practical Implications," 163.

8. Ibid., 165.

9. Name withheld, "Indonesia: The Divine Appointment," in *Partners Together* newsletter, CBInternational, February 2003.

CHAPTER 5
OPEN THEISM AND HOPE

1. All emphases in Scripture references in this paragraph added.

2. John Sanders, *The God Who Risks: A Theology of Providence* (Downers Grove, Ill.: InterVarsity, 1998), 261-262.

CONCLUSION

1. A. W. Tozer, *The Knowledge of the Holy* (New York: Harper & Row, 1961), 11-12.

2. Ibid., 12.

General Index

Abraham: as exemplar of lifelong hope, 120-123; God's informing of about Sodom and Gomorrah, 31; New Testament citation of as a man of faith, 29-30; offering up of Isaac, 25-26, 29-30
affliction. *See* suffering
Alexander the Great, 49
Antiochus IV Epiphanes, 49
"as the Lord had said," 44

Basinger, David, 104
Boyd, Gregory A., 14, 16, 51, 63-65, 70, 79-80, 88, 132n. 11

Caneday, Ardel B., 54, 133n. 14
CBInternational missionary's testimony to answered prayer, 105-106

Cyrus, 38, 49

Daniel 11, details therein as evidence of the reality of God's foreknowledge, 48-50
"David's" story, 109-115
DeArmond, Chelsea, 41, 42
deism, 81

faith, 20-21
false gods, God's indictment of, 22, 36-37
flood, the, 19, 27, 34-35

God: claim to exclusive deity, 18, 38; greatness, goodness, and glory of, 17-19; knowledge and declaration of the future, 36-39. *See also* false gods, God's indictment of; God's

135

foreknowledge; God's
omnipresence; God's
omniscience
God Who Risks, The (Sanders), 19
God's "change of mind," 17, 28,
94-97
God's foreknowledge; biblical
support for God's compre-
hensive and definite foreknowledge, 35-56; biblical
support offered for the open
view of, 25-28; evaluation of
passages used to support the
open view, 29-35; Isaiah's
"big picture" of, 36-39, 132n.
7
God's Lesser Glory (Ware), 7,
131n. 2, 131-132n. 4
God's omnipresence, 31
God's omniscience, 31, 46-48

hope: biblical understanding of,
115-125; for eternity, 123-
125; and God's power, 121-
123; and God's wisdom,
121-123; "living" hope, 124;
for the "long haul," 120-123;
openness view of, 109-115;
for today, 116-120

idolatry, 128
interpretation of Scripture, 56

Jesus' comprehensive claim to
know all things, 53
Jesus' "I am" sayings, 54
Jesus' "Whom do you seek?" 53-
56
Joseph, 21, 62
Judas's betrayal of Jesus, 51

Lewis, C. S., 70
Lord's prayer, 89-91

Moses' intercession for Israel,
94-97

Nebuchadnezzar, 118-119
Ninevites' repentance, 16-17, 40

open theism: basic description
of, 12-13, 81, 127; biblical
claims of, 16-17, 55; and the
book of Daniel, 132-133n. 12;
on decision making, 11; and
"divine growth in knowledge
texts," 131n. 2; and "divine
repentance texts," 131n. 2; as
an "evangelical option," 8; on
human freedom, 12, 15; inordinate estimate of human
self-importance, 100-102; on
the problem of evil, 12, 14-16;
on relationship with God, 13-
14; undermining of the
Christian faith, 19-21; under-

mining of God's greatness, goodness, and glory, 17-19; why open theists believe what they do, 13-17. *See also* God's foreknowledge, biblical support for the open view of; hope, openness view of; prayer, openness view of; prayer, openness works on; prophecy, openness works on; suffering, openness view of

Passover, 42-43
Paul's "thorn in the flesh," 74-76
Peter's denial of Christ, 18, 50-52
Pharaoh's hardened heart, 41-42
plagues, the, 43-44
prayer: biblical understanding of 88-99; difficulties with the openness view of, 99-105; and God's prior knowledge of our needs and hearts' desires, 91-94; and human participation, 98-99; openness view of, 87-88; openness works on, 134n. 1; Paul's prayer about suffering, 74-76; and "your will be done," 89-91, 98. *See also* Lord's prayer
"problem of evil," 12, 14-16, 59

prophecy, 18; "conditional" prophecy, 39-46; openness works on, 132n. 8
Providence and Prayer (Tiessen), 134n. 6
Ptolemy I, 49

regret, and God, 26, 32-34

Sanders, John, 19, 26, 27, 34, 66, 70, 90
Saul, 26-27, 32, 34, 65
Schreiner, Tom, 133n. 14
Seleucus I, 49
self-esteem/self-importance, contemporary overemphasis on, 100-102, 129
"straight" paths, 20-21
suffering: biblical understanding of, 68-76; and character formation, 72-73; giving thanks for, 71-72; as an instrumental good, 69-70; not an essential good, 68-69; openness view of, 11-12, 14-15, 59-60, 63-68, 86; problems with the openness view of, 76-82; rejoicing in, 124-125; seeking deliverance from, 73-76; traditional view of, 59, 60-63, 66-67, 86; use of for the purpose of bringing about some ultimate good, 70-72

Scripture Index

2 Corinthians

1:3-7	70
4:8-12	70
12:1-6	74
12:7-10	74
12:8-10	70
12:9b-10	75

Ephesians

1:4	73
1:11	107
5:20	71

Philippians

3:10	70

1 Thessalonians

5:18	71

2 Timothy

2:13	33
3:12	70

Titus

1:2	33

Hebrews

6:18	33
11	29
11:8-10	29
11:17-19	30
11:19	30
11:36-38	82
12:10	70

James

1:2-4	70, 72
2:21-23	30

1 Peter

1:3-9	123-125

Revelation

21:3-4	69
22:1-5	69